It shouldn't hurt to be a child

NOT ALL SCARS SHOW
NOT ALL WOUNDS HEAL
SOMETIMES YOU
CAN'T ALWAYS SEE
THE PAIN SOMEONE FEELS

According to the National Society for the Prevention of Cruelty to Children (NSPCC):

Approximately 50,500 children in the UK are known to be at risk of abuse right now.

One in four young adults (25.3%) were severely maltreated during childhood.

[June 2012 statistics, www.nspcc.org.uk]

"I am not what
happened to me,
I am what
I choose
to become."

Carl Gustav Jung

"Don't Give Up, Don't Give In"
by Dax Moy
The UK's Leading Holistic Health Coach and Educator

When your heart feels lost within the dark,
When you feel your life has lost its spark,
When you aim your arrows yet they miss their mark,
When your life feels full of lack

When it feels like you can't escape the pain
Or switch off those voices in your brain,
When you watch your joy sliding down the drain,
When life's burdens are breaking your back...

Don't you dare give up, don't you dare give in,
You're closer than you know to finding your win,
You won't go without if you go within,
Just don't give up and don't give in

When it feels like life's become one big fight,
And you feel so weak in the face of might,
When all you want is rest but no end's in sight
When you feel bloodied and bruised and battered

When you're looking for hope but all hope feels lost,
When you doubt what you seek will be worth the cost,
When your heart's begging for warmth but it's covered in frost,
When your heart feels like glass that's been shattered...

Don't you dare give up, don't you dare give in,
You're closer than you know to finding your win,
You won't go without if you go within,
Just don't give up and don't give in

You're so much closer than you think, you know?
And yeah, sometimes the journey feels far too slow,
But each day you hang in and hold on helps you grow,
So much stronger than you were at the start

You're so much more than you seem to be,
If only you could see your reality,
A beautiful soul with a spirit that's free,
Love and light pouring out of your heart

So don't you dare give up, don't you dare give in,
You're so damned close to finding your grin,
To finding the miracle of you that's hidden within,
So don't give up and don't you dare give in.

The Author

I called my book *Through the eyes of a child* for a very specific reason. As a child, you remember things in a certain way. You don't understand what the adults around you are going through themselves, and why should you? You're a kid.

However, as an adult looking back on my childhood experiences and the people around me, I can actually see that there are two sides to a story. As a child, you just remember the event and you remember the feelings and the emotions around that event, but you don't see the bigger picture.

One in four adults have been abused or maltreated as a child and that's a staggering figure, so I'm just trying to bring awareness of abuse and the fact that it is happening behind closed doors. It does need to be brought out and spoken about. It shouldn't be a taboo subject so I'm trying to get people to talk about it.

Ultimately I want the people that are abused to actually realise what abuse is, to understand that what they're going through is not their fault and that they shouldn't have to stay there and suffer in silence and that they should speak to someone that they trust and rely on and when they're ready, they will be able to rely on that person for help to get them out of the situation that they're in.

Chris Tuck

Breaking The Cycle

Survivors Of aBuse

Mel Collie and I have been on many fitness and nutrition courses together and I trusted her enough to read one of the very first versions of *Through the eyes of a child*. Mel and I got chatting and she told me her own story. Her own story of abuse. Since that day, we stayed in contact. I wanted something positive to come out of the book, something more than the book. I shared my ideas with Mel and we brainstormed them all. We wanted to use our experiences and expertise in mindset, nutrition and fitness to help people around the world in similar situations to ourselves. We don't want you to just survive and drag yourself from one day to the next, we want you to thrive and love your life.

Mel and I have co-created the "Breaking The Cycle" C.L.E.A.N. Living Programme; Health For Your Mind & Body.

For further information on "Breaking The Cycle" and how we can help you, please click on the link below:

http://www.survivors-of-abuse.org/

Testimonials

"Your story has moved me beyond words. Such a compelling true story of appalling child abuse, which now, we realise went on but children weren't believed back then.

Look at you now; what an achievement having come from such a violent background. Look at what an amazing life you have worked now, a life you have worked and so hard for and thoroughly deserve.

Your story is a recommended read for everyone in the world who has ever breathed. They will not be able to put it down.

Chris, even if at times you don't feel like it, you are so strong. You pick yourself up and keep going, improving yourself, taking steps to have a better future for your family as well as yourself. Amazing woman. Amazing life.

This book will change your life if you are a survivor of child abuse or know someone who has been through it, and even if you haven't been through abuse yourself, 'Through the eyes of a child' will move you and inspire you. With a proportion of the proceeds going towards children's charities, this book is a worthwhile read, as we all benefit in the end.

I can say so much more! But I do go on a bit! A massive hug and thank you, Chris, for the opportunity to read your story. I'm moved to tears and bless the day I met you at one of Dax Moy's events. I think we chatted in the break at a massive round table drinking herbal tea. What a ride you have been on in your career, lady! Inspirational :)

Here's to the next five, ten, fifteen, twenty years and where it will take you."

Mel Collie

I was screaming and my mum was just like, "No, I've got to go now, I've got to go." But I was pulling at her clothes, "Please stay." She just said, "I can't do this any more. I'll come back for you." And she picked up her suitcase and she just left through the gate.

My dad came out, picked me up, grabbed my brother by the hand and took us into the house. I was crying and screaming my head off. "Where is my mum? Why is she going?" And he just said, "Stop crying, she's gone and that's the end of it. End of." That was it. It was a very, very sad day.

Life was hard after that. Little did we know what was coming our way.

Chris Tuck

Through the eyes of a child

Chris Tuck

Filament Publishing

Published by
Filament Publishing Ltd
16 Croydon Road, Waddon,
Croydon, Surrey CR0 4PA
Telephone +44 (0)20 8688 2598
Fax +44 (0)20 7183 7186
www.filamentpublishing.com
info@filamentpublishing.com

© 2013 Chris Tuck
ISBN 978-1-908691-68-2

Printed by IngramSpark

Contents

This book has been inspired by real events.
Some names have been changed.

Every child in the world is a gift.
Why would you abuse it?

Foreword

I feel very privileged to have been one of the first people to read Christine's journey from an abused and neglected child to the self-assured woman I see today. When I first met Christine, I was struck by her energy, positivity and professionalism. Her demeanour and achievements belie the years of suffering she endured as well as her internal battle to ensure her past did not define her or her future life. Her determination to live a life full of love, hope and compassion, the antithesis of her early experiences is remarkable. I know she will inspire both men and women with a traumatic past to do the same and to work towards reaching their full potential despite the internal scars they bear.

Dr Sarah Cassar
Consultant Psychiatrist

"We wanted and waited for someone, anyone to come and help us but no one came."

Chris Tuck

My story. My memories

"Being unwanted, unloved, uncared for, forgotten by everybody, I think that is a much greater hunger, a much greater poverty than the person who has nothing to eat."

[Mother Teresa]

My name is Chris Tuck. I'm 43, married with two beautiful children and I live in South London.

Most of my clients and acquaintances have no idea of what I've experienced in my life or how easily I could have wound up being just another statistic of child abuse. How for me it wasn't just one or a few isolated incidents, but a tidal wave of neglect, bullying, starvation and survival.

For a long time I've wanted to share my story but didn't feel strong enough. When I first started writing this book about my life, I just wanted to tell my side of it. I wanted to show people what I had been through, how I had coped, and what I had achieved so far in my life.

For all that is still wrong or needs to be changed, I am also very proud of what I have achieved and of who I am.

You see, child abuse never leaves you. You're not supposed to be beaten, touched or starved when you're a child. Mummies and daddies are supposed to love you, not leave you, beat you, or molest your little sister.

When you're a child, your mind is vulnerable. So when you are constantly bullied, put down and told you're worthless by your carers, your teachers, social workers and other kids, your mind gets messed up. You grow up believing it was all your fault. The guilt and sense of blame eat into everything you do and everything you are.

I suppose that's me. Messed up but making something of my life.

No one cared and no one listened. In my world, I became a mum when I was seven.

I remember very little from before then. Maybe I shut it out, I don't know. I have some recollection of the Queen's Silver Jubilee celebration in 1977. Our street had a party. Everyone was having street parties. Our whole street was out celebrating.

All I can remember is that 1977 was the year that changed my life and I can't remember anything, properly, before then.

I can recall little bits but nothing in detail, like getting into trouble for going on railway lines. I can remember getting smacked in front of the whole street for doing stuff like that. I remember that no one ever listened to my side of the story.

I've got about 20 photographs from when I was little, but they don't trigger memories or stories. Even when I look at the photographs, I don't remember anything about them. It's weird. Like I didn't have a childhood.

I can just see this little, skinny kid. I had white hair, like Rod Stewart, except his was cut to look messy; mine just grew like that. My hair seemed to have some afro tendencies in it; it still does. It has a mind of its own. It just grows straight and frizzy right out from my head! It stands up on end.

I always suffered from cold sores too and had big black bags under my eyes.

I'm just a scrap of a thing in those photographs. Hiding, shy, trying to make myself even smaller so no one would notice me. I had zero self-confidence as a child and rarely talked to anyone.

It's all a bit of a muddle. I can't piece things together easily and there are always bits missing. Just a puzzle of memories. Most of them painful. Although if I search really hard, sometimes there's something nice in there. Like the twins I made friends with or the chicken that used to nest in my frizzy, white hair.

I was always angry and frustrated. I wanted someone to notice me and love me but I didn't want to get myself into trouble.

I can't remember dates, just details - probably my brain's way of coping. When I try to remember, I just get snippets of scenes in my mind.

I remember the day my little sister came and found me at work, to tell me that my stepdad had been repeatedly molesting her. We sat in the police room while my sister told the police officer everything he'd made her do. How we'd play hide and seek in the park. How he'd cuddle her into the bushes and make her rub his penis.

I used to be ashamed of who I was and my background. For so long I couldn't tell the world about what I'd been through because of the shame.

I've been trying to write this book for years. I've got notepads with scrawled ideas. Names. Dates. Events. I have endless timelines, all slightly different. When I speak with my siblings, their memories either fill gaps or make things more confusing for me.

Compiling my life story has been tough. I knew I couldn't physically get the words down myself, so I've been putting it all together with the help of a writer, Karen Laing.

When I started writing it all down, it was because I felt like I'd started to get past it. I felt like I had come out of a long, dark and desperate tunnel, and I was now able to show others that no matter what has happened in the past, it doesn't need to dictate your future.

The more I wrote, the more I realised how naive I'd been.

The whole process has thrown up so many issues that I honestly thought I had dealt with. I now realise I still have a long way to go. I've been getting caught up in what people might think and caught up in raw emotions. Writing my story has shown me that I'm still holding on to so many feelings and strong emotions that are holding me back. Holding me back from being truly happy and at peace.

It has shown me that some of my beliefs and behaviours are damaging my relationship with my husband and with myself. So for me, the process of writing this book is a massive milestone, both cathartic and therapeutic.

I've spent my life being put down. Beaten. Told I'll never come to anything. Degraded. But that's not why I'm writing my story. I'm writing my story because I've made something of myself and I really want to tell everyone who's been through stuff like I've been through that you can make something of your life, even though it never truly leaves you.

At the precise moment of writing *Through the eyes of a child*, I realise my feelings and thoughts about particular people in my life are still held strongly in my heart and head as Chris the seven-year-old; Chris the 11-year-old; and Chris the 15-year-old. Although I now understand intellectually that certain people in my life probably did not understand what their actions were doing to me, my emotional self, especially my inner child, has not dealt with the anger and the upset that my siblings and I went through.

All I had done was bury it because it was in the past. I'd always believed that harping on about your past is not going to help you today, or in the future. Is it? Well, perhaps I still have a bit of learning to do.

Going over my story and piecing it together has reminded me of the overwhelming sense of being let down. Let down by so many people. We wanted and waited for someone, anyone to come and help us but no one came.

My brother Dave told me things that we experienced in the past and what we remember in our heads are not the whole story. We've learned that some relatives did try to help but they were unsuccessful.

In my mind, my stepsisters (most of them) were unnecessarily cruel to us. When you read this from my point of view - *Through the eyes of a child* - you will see why. My brother told me that he has spoken to some of my stepsisters recently and their lives have not been happy either.

I truly believe that what I am trying to achieve with my account of my life is to show others my journey from a cruel negative environment to a positive and fulfilling one. I have not sensationalised anything. I have been one hundred percent truthful and factual. I have experienced everything that I have written about. I have, or am, overcoming emotions and feelings that are keeping me in the past. I'm building a better and brighter future.

This story is about cyclical abuse within a family. It includes so many people and even more onlookers who did nothing to help, and I feel guilty about the possibility of hurting others.

For all the neglect and for all those onlookers who didn't help, the process of writing my memories down has helped me to see that there were people who helped and people who were kind. People I need to thank. Their acts of kindness are in this book and are the reason I've made it.

Being honest with myself over the last year it's taken to get this all out has enabled me to truly feel free. This is my story and these are my memories. It doesn't matter who agrees with what I am writing. This is how I feel and these are my views.

I'm going to tell it as I remember it, hoping that it may make more sense to you. Perhaps we can work it out together.

The people that have been in my life, good or bad, have their own stories to tell. They have their own feelings. Their own emotions and demons. They also have the opportunity to tell their own story, if they wish. I am not stopping them.

But now it's time for me to tell *Through the eyes of a child* and to let go.

I've read many books by people who've been abused as I was, like *A Child Called It* by Dave Pelzer. It struck me that in every book I read, the people who wrote them still seem to be plagued by their past. I don't think I am. It's still there and writing it all down has brought out memories I thought were buried, but it doesn't define me anymore.

It doesn't have so much power over me. I've not forgotten it and I don't think I've forgiven either. I've still got a long way to go but I've accepted that it's happened and have chosen to get on with life. I have never chosen to be a victim.

I genuinely believe that I have had a tough time in life but I know without doubt that there are others out there who have it much tougher. I believe that this story of my experiences will inspire others to make changes in their lives. If my story inspires just that one person to get out of a hole, become a success and not be a victim of their birth or circumstances, then it's worth the effort.

This is me laying down my burden. Thank you for reading.

"Child abuse leaves you totally vulnerable to predators. Both people and inner demons."

Chris Tuck

The Beginning

I was born on 17 April 1970 in Chislehurst. I weighed about six pounds, and was long and thin.

I have very few memories before 1977, the year I turned seven.

Before 1977, I was happy. I'm fairly sure of that, although it could have been just normal for our family. My brothers and my sister and I lived in a nice house. We had normal parents; they shouted and fought a lot but we had happy times. We had normal lives, except for the shouting. We lived at 4 Jasmine Grove, Penge and went to Anerley Primary School.

Before 1977, kids didn't pick on us.

One of the first real memories I have is the day my mum left us. The day my mum walked out of the front door and said she couldn't take it anymore; that day is etched in my memory. Even now, at 43, these are some of the hardest memories to face. The pain is always there, but it's always where the story starts.

I know I was always shy and scared. Introverted. I didn't connect well with other children. I vaguely remember Mum dropping me off at nursery and how I would hide under a slide for the whole time I was there. I could have only been three or four. I didn't speak to anyone. Just me, alone with my slide. Hiding.

I can't remember exactly when stuff happened. I just start getting confused with things. I was a kid when most of the beating and starving happened. Time is different when you're a child. Minutes feel like hours, everything is magnified - so when big, bad stuff happens to you when you're a child, you tend to remember it. It's like scary stories and fairy tales, except the troll didn't stay under the bridge in my little world. I just stood on top, trying desperately to fight him off my brothers and sisters.

That's the feeling that overwhelms me the most. I was a child but I was forced to be Mum. My own mum just packed her bags and said she couldn't take anymore. After that the world somehow told me, Chris the seven-year-old, that it was my responsibility now.

Even though I was trying to be Mum, I could never protect my family from grown-ups. Every time I failed, it made me feel worse. I was totally responsible, but totally helpless all at the same time.

We lived near a park called South Norwood Lakes. It had a big tall slide near the railway lines. I used to beg Dad to let us go out and play. It was a bit of a trek from where we lived.

There was a lad called Gary who lived near us. He was a local trouble maker. One day Dad had let us go to the park: Gary, my brother Dave, my sister Diane, some of my stepsisters, our dogs Pip and Patch and some other local children from the estate all trekked up to the park.

David, Diane, me and our dogs Pip and Patch were playing on the big slide. We could see Gary and two of my stepsisters through a big hole in the fence with a group of kids from our streets. They were playing chicken with the trains - jumping on and off the railways lines and laughing.

I remember feeling really scared. Of Gary. Of my stepsisters. Of the other kids. Of the trains. Dad had told us to stay safe and out of trouble, but Gary kept calling us over. I didn't want to go.

Eventually he took my hand and led us to the other kids. I didn't want to go. He showed us how to step over the railway lines carefully. I didn't want to.

Our dogs were loyal and they followed us. Patch trod on the line and was electrocuted. The noise he made was hideous. I thought I was going to be sick. Suddenly I didn't want to play anymore and I started to cry. Shocked, terrified and guilty. I felt like it was my fault. We fled back into the park.

We didn't know that a train driver had contacted the police. The police were running towards us as we were climbing back through the fence. Gary and the gang were running off in all directions. We just stood there. The police took us home.

Dad was beyond angry. He was a violent man, especially when he got angry, but I suppose this was just normal to us. That's how dads were.

I can remember being told off by Dad and Vivien in front of everyone. He put both Dave and then me over his knee in turn and smacked us, to show everyone that what we'd done was wrong. He told us we needed to learn a lesson. We would always need to learn a lesson.

It was Gary who had led us astray and he never got punished - something I'd learn was just the way things would be. Like Vivien's kids, they were the same. The family we ended up living with after Mum left us. Our stepsisters. I can tell you Cinderella's ugly sisters were angels compared to the abuse we got from them.

That's the thing about child abuse and neglect. Unless you've been through it, you don't really get it. When you are constantly beaten and put down at home, you crave attention elsewhere. So you get into trouble. Like the man who was kind to me, who used to give me sweets whilst he groomed me.

Child abuse leaves you totally vulnerable to predators. Both people and inner demons.

Child abuse does not stop with the child. It affects their relationships, their siblings and their families. Without help, it repeats itself. Kids learn behaviours. It's tough to unlearn them.

Take my brother Dave. In spite of all we went through, he ended up in the family courts. He used to shout at his wife and kids so much that his neighbours called in social services. Dave is a beautiful man. He was depressed and fighting so many of his own demons.

By the time I was 16 I'd moved home eight times, changed families twice, lived in a tent in Wales for six months and ended up in the local homeless unit three times.

I've seen a child die. Little David, with his white blonde hair and sparkling blue eyes, who fell and dashed his brains out on the concrete. It took me a long time to realise it wasn't my fault, that there was no way I could have caught him and saved him.

We moved schools many times. Sometimes we didn't go to school. We were malnourished, beaten, tormented, and I've learned first hand that school kids can be really cruel when you go to school smelly with holey clothes.

Do you remember those kids at school? The smelly, weird kids. The ones who looked like they never washed, or brushed their teeth or hair. The ones no one talked to. I was one of those kids. I wanted toothpaste. I wanted soap. I longed for shoes that didn't have holes in them - ours were patched together with scraps of newspaper. Any money my stepmum got from the social went straight to her kids or to her cigarette habit. We had more than nothing because to add to the starvation and neglect, we were beaten, mocked and tormented.

I shared a room and a bed with my sister Diane and two stepsisters but my little brother Michael was always scared and cried himself to sleep, so we would take it in turns to get into bed with him to make him feel better.

We used to smell of wee most of the time because Diane and Michael wet the bed. My little brother was two and my sister was four when my mum left us.

When they wet the bed, they were beaten. So out of fear they'd wet the bed more. Vivien used to rub their noses in their sheets. They learned to hide their wet clothes and sheets.

Michael was still wetting the bed when my mum finally got custody of us four years later.

Diane has told me recently that she and Michael were beaten every day for fun. She is so affected and traumatised by what has happened that she is currently undergoing a psychiatric assessment and treatment. At 41, she is still experiencing harrowing flashbacks and nightmares. As we speak, Diane is finally getting the expert help she needs to move on with her life.

Sunday Fish Buffets and a Happy Christmas

I remember our Sunday fish buffets when I was six or seven. It was all cockles, toothpicks and shiny fireplaces.

I've always been an early riser and on Sundays my mum and dad would have a lie in. This was before Mum left and when things were all okay between Mum and Dad (or so it seemed to us).

One day I was waiting for them to wake up. I was bored and I noticed our fireplace was dirty. I got a duster, cleaning spray and got down on my knees. I've always been one of those types who wanted to be busy, who wanted to be useful and help people.

At that age, all I wanted to do was please my parents. They would shout and argue a lot but to us that was just normal. I suppose because they were always angry and tense, I wanted to please.

I cleaned the chrome and the marble surround until it was so shiny I could see my face in it. All big eyes and frizzy haired, little Chris staring back at me, upside down. It was really funny. It took forever to clean but it looked really good and I was so proud.

When Mum woke up, I showed her the fireplace. She took one look at it and there was nothing but praise for how lovely it looked. In those days doing something useful meant praise.

So every week that became my little job. I'd get up early to clean and polish the fireplace and every Sunday teatime I'd sit next to it when we had our fish tea. We had buttered bread and bowls of cockles. I'd sit, transfixed, fishing the tiny, acidic little cockles and winkles out of their shells with a pin.

Cleaning the fireplace to make Mum proud of me felt like I was taking some of the burden away from her and our family. I was so little but I felt an overwhelming need to fix everything, to take charge and try to look after my family.

I can remember the Christmas before Mum left too. It's one of those really happy memories that I have to dig hard for but it's there. My brain won't let it go.

My little sister Diane, who would have been four, and I had been looking all round the house for our Christmas presents. We couldn't find anything and we were getting really upset and cross. Perhaps if we'd known what Christmases would be like in the future, we'd have behaved a bit differently but at the time it was so important. Eventually Mum and Mad gave us a clue and in the cupboard in the hallway was a present each.

When we opened them up, all we found was a toy parasol. We were livid. We'd been tricked! It seemed like a mean joke to play on two excited little girls. Then Mum and Dad showed us to a massive pile of presents stashed underneath the fish tanks in the front room. We each had a baby doll dressed completely in hand-knitted clothes. Mum and Nan had knitted all the clothes by hand. Mine was pink, Diane's was blue. We also had a double buggy each that our parasols fitted onto.

I remember that Christmas well; it is etched on my brain like it was yesterday. We were happy. We had a proper Christmas. It's the last one I remember.

Those memories flash into my brain every time I'm given a Christmas present. I still cry sometimes when someone gives me a gift. The kindness of others is often too hard to bear.

How quickly my mind shifts back to 1977. The year Mum left. The year life fell apart, the shit started and life changed completely.

My entire little world was shattered.

This is where my story really begins.

"Each of the agencies involved blamed each other.

They promised that 'lessons would be learnt'.

But it still continues."

Chris Tuck

1977

Jasmine Grove was one of London's mixed-up streets. We saw all types of life when we were growing up but our little family was our world and sanctuary - it was safe. All sorts lived in our neighbourhood, from the squatters near Oakfield Road, to the Allens at number seven.

The Allens. Lauded over by matriarch Vivien. A vicious, evil woman. As ugly as she was wicked. The archetypal fairy tale witch. She had wiry hair and little stubs for teeth. She was so ugly. Maybe she was a witch. She had smoke lines around her mouth, like she'd held on to a brown fag stub in her skinny, old wrinkly lips all her life.

Vivien had seven children. Her youngest was five months older than me.

1977 was the first year any of us ever saw our parents fight, or maybe the first time I remembered seeing it. All I can remember is in that year, Dad started spending a lot more time at number seven Jasmine Grove than he did at number four.

Some days, when David and I came home from school, Mum would say, "Go and get your dad for his dinner." We always knew where to go and fetch him. He was always in the back room of number seven. He'd be lying on the settee reading a book.

"Dad? Mum says tea's ready."

"You kids run along," he'd grunt, irritated. "I'll come home when I'm good and ready."

This seemed to be the only dialogue between my mum and dad for a long time until the day she walked out.

Dad had upset her. She quickly packed clothes into suitcases, tears streaming down her face. She kissed me goodbye. I can remember asking where she was going. I was screaming. I was seven. I remember the warm, wet, salty tears on our faces. It's one of the most raw memories I own. It changed everything.

"Why are you going?" I sobbed.

"I have to go. I can't stay," she managed to get out between gasps. I'd never seen Mum like this. My rock. My mum. "I'll be back soon." But she wasn't.

With that, we watched our mum walk out of the door, through the front garden gate and down the length of Oakfield Road.

We'd gone from shiny fireplaces and cockle picking with toothpicks to screaming, and Mum leaving us all with a little, battered up suitcase in her hand. She never looked back to see us - or at least, that's how I remember it; through my eyes.

Mum's leaving started a catalogue of being let down. My shit parents. All those people who should have helped us but didn't.

I just stood there. Seven years old. My brother David was eight, Diane was five and my little brother Michael just two. We wanted our mummy.

Vivien. My stepmother. The witch

After Mum left, we all moved in together in Jasmine Grove. Well, Dad and Vivien lived in our house and all the kids lived in Vivien's old house. We used to come and go as we pleased between the two houses.

Eventually we all ended up together after one of my stepsister's burned the backs of her legs when her skirt caught fire on an old electric heater. I can remember running, screaming down the road, shouting out that she was on fire.

My memories of Vivien are all bad. I have no idea what motivated her to be so cruel. To me, she was greedy, lazy and malicious. She'd be worse when my dad wasn't around.

Vivien hit us, often, with anything she could find, usually in front of her own kids to degrade us. She put us down constantly and set us up for her beatings. Nothing we did was ever good enough for Vivien. If we got upset, she laughed.

She was a nasty little woman. Everything about her was brown, shrivelled and tar stained from her endlessly smoking her way through our benefits.

There was no caring, no nurture. Vivien made sure she did just enough to keep the authorities off her back so she could keep us and our benefits.

She delighted in telling us that she only really kept us for that money. Later, when my mum would try to get custody of us, Vivien would come home and tell us that she was pleased Mum didn't get us back because it would mean losing our benefit money - benefit money we never saw.

Life when I was eight went something like this: I'd have porridge for breakfast. Porridge made with water. Porridge so salty that you could barely stomach it. We got school dinners and that was it.

I can remember being sent to our rooms straight after school without food. We'd watch all the other kids in the street playing. Tea was only ever a slice of bread and butter but when we were punished we didn't get that. We were always hungry so our bellies would grumble even more when we were punished.

On the nights we weren't sent straight to our rooms we did chores, like sweeping the stairs or scrubbing the floors.

We had to clean the house from top to bottom. We had to take our time over the chores. Vivien would inspect our efforts and if it wasn't done to her satisfaction then we would have to redo it until it was. If it wasn't right the first time, we'd get more cleaning jobs to do and then we'd get punished. It was never done right first time.

We were always punished. Vivien and her kids would set us up for punishment. I'm sure that's why I became so devious. Vivien would get her kids to spy on us and tell her when we did anything wrong so that she could beat us.

If we weren't doing chores or being punished, we would be told to get lost after breakfast and not to come back until teatime. We often came back cold and wet but Vivien wouldn't let us in until she was ready. She would just stand at the window laughing at us, making fun of us shivering and sniffling outside.

When I think about it, I can be right back under Vivien's control in my memories. I'm there sweeping the stairs with a dustpan and brush. Vivien inspects it. It's not good enough. I do it again. It's still not good enough. She raps me over the knuckles. Now I have to redo the stairs from top to bottom. I have sore knuckles. I am sobbing my heart out and she is laughing. Laughing at my pain.

If my punishments weren't painful enough, every time my siblings got punished it felt worse to me. I used to get so upset. I physically felt their pain. I still do.

I was upset all the time because I wasn't able to protect my family from the torment. I became emotional because of the beating and bullying my brothers and sister were dealt. The mind games were tiring. They still are. Many times I just wanted to give up but something deep down always kicked in and made me face what was happening.

We were always miserable. Trapped. It felt like there was no way out. Constantly living on our nerves. Wondering what was going to happen next. Wondering where our next meal was coming from.

We'd share beds for comfort. We cuddled up for warmth. When I shared a bed with my little sister, she had fidgety feet. It used to annoy me. I used to kick her really hard, something I now regret!

We were constantly told we were ugly and stupid and that no one loved us. Vivien would always compare us to her children, telling us how different we were, how wonderful her children were and how much she loved them. Not like us.

This was her sick joke. I have since discovered Vivien didn't care for her own children either. Before we came along, she neglected their basics needs too. We were fresh blood for her, and her girls were probably pleased that her attention was now on other children and not them.

My hair used to stick up like an Afro. Vivien and her children used to taunt me about it. Dad just sat back and said nothing.

"You're thick."

"You smell."

"You're ugly."

"No one will ever want you."

So that was what we believed. It was all we heard as children, at home and at school. When social services got involved, they never believed our stories. If it wasn't for the fact that we knew Mum was out there somewhere, we'd have grown up with absolutely zero sense of self-worth.

We were starved. Starved of love and starved of food.

Vivien's kids picked on us all the time. They'd gang up on us and watch us when we got beaten.

I remember once how one of my stepsisters asked to borrow my silver, heart-shaped signet ring. It was only a cheap ring but my Nan had bought it for me just before Mum left. It was the only pretty thing I owned and it meant the world to me. I think it must have cost less than a tenner from Argos but I treasured it. My ring was something Vivien could never take off me because it was tight on my finger! It was a reminder that somewhere my Mum and my Nan were waiting to get us back.

My two younger stepsisters asked if they could try it on. I said no. Then Judy, my stepsister, asked me. She said she was going on a trip and wanted to borrow it for the day. "I'll look after it," she'd said. I remember making my finger red raw trying to get the ring off my finger but I trusted Judy. She was nice to us and I wanted to please her - and there was always the threat of another trick and another beating by Vivien, so I gave in and let her borrow it. I never saw the ring again.

We brushed our teeth with salt water, then we went to bed. Hungry. No lights on. I can remember reading books by street lamps. I can remember the burst blood vessel in my eye from eye strain, which I still have now.

The physical, mental and emotional abuse I suffered under Vivien's rule led to rock-bottom self-esteem. I was always on the lookout for being picked on or reprimanded for things I hadn't done, or ready to spring to the rescue for my brothers and Diane. I learned to watch my back. I had to. As I child I would stand against the wall, to try to fade into the background. I never wanted to draw attention to myself unless it was to get food.

In social situations I often stand with my back against a wall. I don't like anyone to walk or stand behind me; I need to see what they are doing.

In school or at college, I would often sit at the end of a row so that I could see what was going on and escape if necessary. I've just finished studying for my ITEC massage exams, and during the lessons I always sat on the end of the row. My course mates noticed and asked me about it. I laughed it off and said it's just one of my habits! I'm 43 but I still need to know I'm not trapped, that I can escape if necessary. There is nothing worse for me than the feeling of being trapped in a corner with no way out.

Of all the shit we faced, it's the overwhelming hunger that stands out. Even now as I write this, I am eating nuts! I am not hungry, I am just trying to fill an emotional black hole.

I can't remember ever feeling full when I was a child. I was always hungry. It was constant, maybe that's why so many memories are about food.

We didn't ever have fruit, vegetables or treats. We had no money for lunch when we weren't at school. Even at secondary school, where we got dinner tickets, I would often sell mine to other pupils, in spite of the hunger. It wasn't because I was greedy but because I was always saving money for an emergency. An escape route. Money meant freedom and control - perhaps that's why I became an accountant!

We were scavengers and beggars. We used to pick up McDonald's leftovers from the floor, or we'd wait outside the Chatterton chip shop in the hope that customers would feel sorry for us and treat us to some chips. In the winter it was warm so we hung around for heat, and the owner used to give us portions of chips just to make us go away.

We were hungry but we still felt ashamed at our begging and stealing.

In primary school, after lunch when no one was around, I would raid the bins for apple cores that the other kids had thrown away. I would ask to go to the toilet after playtime and I would eat the cores and the seeds secretly before going back to class. It was always in a hurry, just in case I got caught. Even now I have an obsession with apples. I have to eat the whole thing.

I had a friend who used to have a packed lunch. Every day she brought a big red, shiny apple into school for break. It was so shiny and I was so hungry. I'm sure I probably used to stare at it. So one day she noticed me looking at her eating it and the next day she bought an extra one in for me. When she saw me eat it so quickly, ravenously hungry, she went home and told her mum. From that day on, I was given an apple every day by my friend.

One day she was ill and I can remember when the teacher told me I got really upset. Then my friend's mum came to school. She came into my class and gave me the apple. She must have realised how much I needed it.

Perhaps it was those little acts of kindness that got me through, that stopped me from giving up on life.

*

In the garden of our house in London Road, Dad had a massive aviary. He had budgies at the top and rabbits at the bottom. One day, one of the pet rabbits jumped up and killed a few of the budgies. I remember Dad got mad about it. His blasted budgies.

That night, we sat at the dinner table and I can remember Dad and Vivien laughing about the meal. They asked us to taste the meat. We took a mouthful. Dad handed us something furry. He told us it was a good luck charm. A rabbit's foot.

We were eating our pet rabbits for tea.

It was perhaps the most wicked thing they'd ever done, especially since they were so excited about telling us. Laughing at our disgust; making us the butt of their awful joke. At first we wouldn't believe him so he told us to go down to the basement and look for ourselves.

Diane and I crept down the stairs, into the damp, cold, dark of the basement. We hated going down there; it was dingy and creepy and the smell caught in the hairs of your nostrils. Only today, in the dark of our basement, there was a different smell. Instinctively we knew Dad and Vivien weren't tricking us and as our eyes adjusted to the dark, we could just make out the two pet rabbits strung up, their dead eyes staring at us, their limp ears hanging down to the floor!

We screamed, shaking and horrified from the thought, but the more we squealed and cried, the greater delight the adults took in our distress. Dad, Vivien and her eldest children, just laughing at us.

It wasn't long after that my little sister Diane was taken to hospital for malnutrition. They tried to feed her meat. She gagged. They thought she was being difficult. At the time I knew about the rabbit but there was other stuff I'd find out later, other reasons she wouldn't eat and kept quiet. Neither Dad nor Vivien ever bothered to go and visit her but I would walk five miles each way to the hospital. It took me about an hour and a half each day, each way. On my own. I was eight but she was my little sister and I loved her.

Diane still has eating issues and struggles eating meat. She still remembers the day with the rabbits in the basement and them all laughing. She can't eat any meat that has a face.

Sweets. The candy man

There was a man who used to park his passenger transit van near our house. He used to come and talk to all of the kids and hand out sweets. He let us sit on the bonnet of his van.

I was always hungry, bullied by the other kids at school, constantly put down and degraded at home, beaten. Then there was this man, who was nice, who gave me sweets. This man who made me feel really special.

That's the thing about child abuse. I understand it more now. It's not just about the physical pain and starvation, or the mental torment and constant bullying, there was plenty of that. It's also about vulnerability and a huge need for love and attention. I wasn't getting love from my parents. Mum had left, my stepmum was an abusive witch and my dad just left her to it.

As an abused child, you look different. You act different, and so you get bullied by kids too. You are always looking for happiness, for someone to show kindness. When someone does show you attention, it feels really special, even if his motives are based in his crotch. You are the child that a paedophile preys on, the 'vulnerable child' people talk about in the news.

I used to show off to all the other kids who liked to call us names. I used to tell them that this man was my friend. I used to boast to them, "You can't come up here, this is a special van."

This man lived in a bedsit on Plaistow Lane. One day he invited me, one of my stepsisters and another child back to his bedsit. I don't remember how we got there. Dad and Vivien always wanted us to get lost so we had plenty of opportunity. They never asked where we went.

I don't remember the house. I just remember he lived in a downstairs flat and I remember from the minute I walked in the house I felt scared.

I remember him saying, "If you just come inside, I'll give you some sweets." Then it was, "If you just sit down, I'll give you some sweets." It didn't feel right but I didn't know why and I didn't know what to do.

I remember him putting the TV on and telling us to sit in front of it.

He called us to him one at a time... I turned my back to the TV so I couldn't see what was going on. I knew that whatever he was doing, it wasn't right...I was scared...when it was my turn, he called me over.

He was lying down on the sofa and he showed me something. When I saw it, I knew it was wrong. This nice man with the transit van bonnet and the sweets was showing me his penis.

He asked me what it was and I told him I didn't know. He asked me if I would like to touch it. I said no. He told me if I touched it, he'd give me some sweets. I said no. He grabbed my hand and made me stroke him. I didn't like it. I didn't want it. It made me feel sick. This nice man with the sweets. The transit van bonnet. The bedsit. The TV. The penis. I'd said no. I took my hand away and told him I wanted to go home now.

I was a child, probably about nine, I don't remember exactly. This man was making me stroke his penis. He'd given me sweets and had been kind to me when no one else was, but he was making me do something horrible. I didn't understand it but I knew it was wrong. He was making me do something that would make me never want to touch a penis again. He was making me do something that would scar me forever.

I still drive past that house and shudder - that man pops into my head. The memory is always there, like the house that never goes. It's one of those memories I cannot bury.

He tried to placate us by giving us sweets, he told us not to tell anyone and then he would let us go home. When we agreed, we left the bedsit and ran all the way home.

All I can remember is feeling dirty. I felt disgusting. Every time I saw his van, I wouldn't go near it. We didn't tell anyone straight away about it but we started telling people not to go near the man with the transit van and sweets.

I was scared to say anything because I thought I'd be in trouble. I knew that going with strangers was wrong and I was sure I'd be beaten if they found out, but we must have been acting really strange because soon after I remember someone asking why we were so upset. It was maybe days or weeks later but I remember we told Vivien and Dad all about it.

They called the police and we were questioned at Bromley Police Station. I remember being examined by the doctor to make sure that we hadn't been raped.

The internal examination was horrendous. In many ways, worse than the man making me stroke his penis. No one was allowed to come with me. The police woman explained to me what would happen but I didn't really understand. She laid me down and checked my vagina. I'd never felt so vulnerable or so alone.

I remember crying, feeling ashamed and hurting.

Wales

I remember that we were always broke. Vivien never worked. My dad was a carpenter but never seemed to work. We'd always be getting letters about rent money due or running out of money in the meters. They always struggled to find 50p's for the gas and electricity.

One day, Dad came home with this blue Bedford Commer van. He was really excited. It was an old rust bucket of a van that didn't look like it could even reach the end of the street.

He got all us kids together and told us we were going on an exciting trip - that we were leaving 98 London Road and going to Wales! Dad and Vivien told us we were going to leave late at night one day soon, so the neighbours wouldn't see us leaving and the council couldn't find us. It didn't mean much to us at the time but it sounded like a massive adventure, and it would be.

One night we were all bundled into this van and told to keep quiet. Dad and Vivien had emptied all the money from the meters inside the house. We set off in our van loaded with mattresses, clothes, kids, coats, blankets, cooking utensils and two dogs and we left. Just left.

We drove all night in the blue van. Dad kept going on about driving within the speed limits because he didn't want the police to stop us. The van wasn't insured or taxed and the tyres were so bald that every time we went round a corner, the wheel arches would screech. I remember we had to stop often to allow the radiator to cool down and top it up with cold water.

Eventually we arrived at Gwen Farm, Merthyr Tydfil, South Wales.

The farmhouse was at the top of the farm near the entrance. Our tents were pitched down the hill in a field near a horse paddock.

We had two tents. A big one that had two bedrooms and a living area, and a small one. The youngest kids, eight of us, were bundled together in the small tent. The only thing keeping us warm was each other and our coats. It was uncomfortable and cold. Really cold.

The only place to wash and go to a proper toilet was up at the farmhouse, where there was an outside toilet. We used to walk up the hill in the morning to go to the toilet and wash in cold water before walking to school. Once a week we used to get a big grey plastic tub in the main tent and have a proper wash down.

If we wanted to go to the toilet at night-time, we would just go outside the tent in the dark. It was freezing outside and dark and scary. There were only children in our small tent, so I would have to get out of my tiny space, step over other bodies and try to find the tent entrance in pitch black. I often ended up treading on someone or waking the others up and getting into trouble.

There were other tents all around us. We must have been quite a novelty on that Welsh campsite! Four adults with all those kids. We ended up living on the farm in tents for over six months; we even went to a school in the main town for a while. It was uncomfortable and cold but I've got lots of happy memories of Wales.

The school in Wales was really different to our English school. I found it hard to make friends. We were outsiders. They had a whole different language. For a start they called plimsolls, dabs. All the Welsh children ate this strange fruit called pomegranate and played strange Welsh games in the playground.

I soon learned to love pomegranates. I used to spend hours picking the individual seeds out with a pin!

The school used to run competitions for writing stories and poetry. Every week the winners would be called out in assembly and would win a packet of crisps. I entered every competition, every week to make sure I won a packet of crisps.

At this school all the kids were given a bottle of milk every day. Loads of kids didn't like their milk so we used to be given extra.

I remember the class being split into tables and depending on how bright you were, you were put on the table near the door and it worked its way back to the table being near the teacher for those who were struggling. I was on this table. I think this was the first time I was aware that I was behind with my education.

My dad was called to the school and asked to give me extra tuition at home. I remember sitting on the hilltop in the summer sun being taught maths by my dad and understanding his lessons less than I understood the whole plimsolls dabs stuff!

The farmhouse used to sell some provisions for the guests on the farm. The lady at the farmhouse used to sell packets of biscuits for 50p. We would often get sent to the farmhouse to buy biscuits for Dad and the other grown-ups, but we were hungry which made us devious. While the farm lady went to get change, we stole some biscuits for ourselves. We knew it was wrong but we were hungry.

It didn't take the farmhouse lady long to figure out what was going on but she was kind. She realised we were hungry and would give us extra biscuits. She told us to eat them before we got back to the tent!

The farm lady had a physically handicapped daughter. She would often invite us in to play with her. Every time we went to play, she fed us. I can remember the farm lady asking us to wash our hands and face before eating. I can only assume we were all very dirty! She would feed us and spend time with us. They were happy times on the farm.

We used to help out with the sheep dipping on the farm too. One poor sheep was riddled with maggots; it was the first time I'd seen anything like it. Its fleece was moving and it stank. The farmer put the poor thing down on the spot.

We used to spend ages roaming through the fields, chasing the horses around and scrumping fruit from the trees.

I can remember making friends with a horse on the farm. We called him Goblin. It would chomp its teeth, and for ages after my brothers and sisters nicknamed me Goblin because of the way I chomped my teeth when I slept.

I made friends with a one-legged chicken too. I called it Hoppity! I used to have really frizzy, untamed hair and Hoppity loved to fly up, jump on my head and make a nest in it! She'd sit there forever. When we eventually moved back to London, Hoppity the one-legged, nest-making chicken came with us - but she was never destined to be a city chicken – as she soon became breakfast for a South London fox.

One day, when my sister and I were having our weekly wash in the big grey tub, my dad and Vivien told us that my Nanny Andrews who had diabetes had died. Nanny Andrews was a kind lady and used to love us visiting her.

Nanny Andrews lived with Uncle Frank in Mottingham. She was bedridden. Her diabetes had led to her having her leg amputated. She used to have a big pet spider called Charlie who lived on her wall by her bed.

We were really upset at the news. Nanny Andrews had been someone who cared about us. A lifeline.

Years later, we would find out that Nanny Andrews and Uncle Frank had known what was going on with our family but weren't in a position to be able to help. We missed Nanny Andrews.

While we lived on the farm, we had lots of jobs to do. One of these jobs was sawing wood. My dad had a great big saw with big jagged teeth. One day I pestered him so much to let me have a go that he eventually did, but the saw slipped and I ended up sawing my finger down to the bone at the knuckle. "I told you so," he said as blood pumped absolutely everywhere. I've still got the scar on my knuckle!

Then one day, out of the blue, Dad and Vivien disappeared. We didn't know where they were going or when they'd be back. They left us with one of our eldest stepsisters and her boyfriend. We had no food and no money, so we started stealing from other tents. We didn't know this at the time but the other tent occupants complained and so the nice lady at the farmhouse told us we had to leave.

The stealing is still really hard for me to admit to and accept. I still think we were in the wrong.

We used to steal money too. I'm still ashamed to admit it, but we did it because we were truly hungry. It wasn't like the girls at school who used to go shoplifting for the latest fashionable clothes. We were starving.

Later on, we would steal money from Vivien too. She would leave small amounts of change around the house to tempt us. She would wait for some to go missing, which it invariably did, and then took great delight in punishing us. Sometimes we stole the money, sometimes my stepsisters stole it but often it was Vivien!

I've only recently found out from one of my stepsisters, Tracey, what really happened to us in Wales. Vivien and Dad had tried to get us housing in Wales but the Welsh authorities knew about our house in Bromley, the one we'd fled from, and told them to go back to Bromley to get re-housed. So that's why Dad and Vivien left us all, in a tent, in the middle of winter. They just drove back to Bromley.

It took them 24 hours to get back to Bromley because the radiator in the old van kept on overheating.

When they got back, Vivien's eldest daughter, Tracey, who was still in Bromley, found out what they'd done. When she found out that they had left us to fend for ourselves with no money, in the middle of winter, Tracey's husband Alan jumped straight in their car and drove to Wales to rescue us.

They found us scared, cold, dirty and hungry.

Alan drove us back to their flat in Bromley. They bathed us, fed us and put us to bed. It was soon after this that we were all re-housed to Stanley Road in Bromley after a stint in John Baird House, the homeless unit in Penge.

"Childhood should be carefree, playing in the sun; not living a nightmare in the darkness of the soul."

Dave Pelzer
author of *A Child Called 'It'*

Life after Wales

When we got back from Wales, we went to St Mark's Primary School. I was the thickest in the class but at least I wasn't put back a year.

I still wrote stories. I'd write about all the stuff that was going on, pretending it was about someone else. The teachers would ask if it was true. We said it was but they didn't believe us.

After Wales, life was far more unsettled. It was just a cycle of running out of money, moving and hiding from the council. On one occasion when we ran out of money, Vivien burned our house down.

I'd spent ages making one of those pyjama case covers. It was a doll on the outside and had a secret compartment on the inside. We'd made them at school and I'd taken so much pride in making mine; it was a labour of love. I didn't own anything special but I had this pretty thing I'd made that no one could take away and I hung it proudly in the window of our bedroom.

It was the day of Charles and Diana's wedding. Vivien told us we were all going out for a picnic. She packed us up and we walked from Bromley to Keston with the dogs, Pip and Patch. We had a fun day, which was strange in itself! We didn't do nice things with Vivien! Vivien usually told us to get lost and here we were eating, altogether in the park for the whole day. Everyone was out celebrating because of the wedding.

When we got back, there were two fire engines in our road. Our house was engulfed in flames and smoke. My pyjama doll case was hanging up at the window with flames licking up at it. I was devastated. I didn't care much for the house but I did care for that pyjama doll case ... and it was all Vivien's fault.

Everything was Vivien's fault. I hated this woman for everything. No one can imagine how low and insignificant this woman made me feel. How lonely I felt. How unloved I felt. How uncared for I felt. At the time, I could not do anything about it. I just thought, "Where is my mum?"

Here I am at the age of 43. The pain of how she made me feel is still as raw, at times, as it was then.

Peek-a-boo little David

After the fire, we were moved to John Baird House in Penge. John Baird House was a homeless unit.

While we were there, social workers would come and talk with us. They'd take us off, one at a time. One at a time, we'd tell them what was going on - exactly what was going on, and one at a time, they didn't believe us.

When the social workers came around, Vivien would make sure she dressed us in our smartest clothes. We'd all sit at the table, eat dinner and make it look like we were a happy family.

Vivien would always tell us that it didn't matter what we said, the social workers would always believe the adults over the children, so in the end we stopped trying. We knew that to Vivien and Dad, we were nothing. We were picked on at school because of the way we looked and picked on at home because we were there. The social workers didn't listen and our school teachers didn't believe us. We ended up thinking we were nothing and that there was no way out. Downtrodden and hopeless.

However it was those little glimmers of hope that made me end up differently to the rest of my family. The girl at school with the apple. Friends who stuck by me. The lady at the farmhouse. Those little acts of kindness that have stuck fast to my psyche. It's like that old saying, remember the little things because one day you'll look back and remember they were the big things!

John Baird House was made up of eight maisonettes on the first floor and eight on the ground floor. You had one maisonette per family, or two or three families shared.

The main entrance was to the front of the building and all the front doors overlooked the concrete courtyards and garages. Railings ran up the stairs and along the first floor, but the railings were too wide to be safe - big enough for a toddler to fit through. While we were living there made, something happened, something that made them change those big, wide railings.

We used to play games down on the concrete by the garages underneath the first floor corridor. All the kids living in the shelter would play out together. At the time there were two little boys called David and Gavin. David was a lovely, angelic looking boy with blonde hair. He was the apple of his mum's eye but his brother Gavin was constantly picked on.

One day David was playing peek-a-boo through the railings on the first floor. He kept on poking his head through those railings. We started to get scared because he thought it was fun, but the railings were too wide and he was high up. High up over a concrete floor.

We started shouting at him not to do it and calling out for his mum. I told David to go and find his mum hoping that it would make him stop playing the peek-a-boo game, but because we were talking to him and he was getting our attention, he wouldn't stop.

He pushed himself through the railings and let go. We ran over to where we thought he was going to land to try to catch him.

He landed on his back. His head was cracked open from the fall.

We screamed for help but no one came.

We all gathered around him. Staring down. Helpless. Just kids.

David looked up smiling with blood and fluid leaking from his head. We tried to stop him. We tried to catch him, but that beautiful blonde head of hair was cracked and brown with blood.

David died from his injuries.

After David's death, the council made the railings solid.

Since that day, anything involving heads really turns my stomach. It makes me think about David. I often think about David, the angelic little boy with beautiful blonde hair playing peek-a-boo through the railings.

Gavin was always picked on and worse by his mum and I couldn't help thinking at the time that Gavin was going to have a shit life. It wasn't his fault. It used to make me feel really sad.

"Abuse of any kind is destructive, soul destroying and wrong."

Chris Tuck

Dad the paedophile

We came home from school one day to find the house empty of the usual nine children, just my dad sitting on the sofa. My sister Diane had been kept off school so she wouldn't be involved. But my two brothers, Michael and David, and I came home as usual to find Dad just sitting there reading a book, like it was any other day.

We were used like pawns. We had to come home as normal so Dad wouldn't guess anything was up.

I later found out from my stepsister Tracey that Vivien, her daughters and Diane went to her flat that day.

The police knocked down the door, charged the house and handcuffed my dad - in front of my brothers and I. I was screaming at the police asking them to let my dad go.

It wasn't until I went back to school, after he was arrested and all the kids taunted me in the playground saying, "Your dad's a paedo," that I'd even heard of the word. I didn't know what being a paedophile meant at that age but my dad was one. The police woman just said, "Your dad has been a very naughty man."

Vivien later told us that she'd had to go to the police to protect my sister, Diane. She'd caught him in bed, at it, with some of my stepsisters.

The process of writing this book has led to lots of deep talking with my eldest stepsister, Tracey.

Tracey, like me, was the eldest girl and had therefore always felt in some way responsible for her siblings. We have a real connection and she has helped me piece together bits of what went on in our families. It's not pretty.

After meeting with Tracey recently, I can now see through my adult eyes that my stepsisters really had no choice but to play along with their mum's instructions in order to protect and survive themselves. As an adult, you can rationalise and make sense of stuff that happened. Tracey told me that her sisters blamed us for our dad abusing them. I never knew this but this makes perfect sense to me now.

We were all children at the time; we were all trying to survive the best way we could. Tracey says her sisters are caring and loving people; we never experienced this because they were under the rule of Vivien. This proves how adults can manipulate young and vulnerable children to do mean and horrible things.

I could never work out why Dad had split from Mum and gone to live with Vivien, 10 years his senior. In hindsight the attraction probably had more to do with my stepsisters.

Dad was convicted for several counts of sexual assault and sentenced to three years in prison. He only ever served 18 months.

Tracey believes the midnight escape to Wales had a lot to do with the abuse. Apparently one of the girls was planning to tell someone about it, which spooked both my dad and Vivien. It was around this time I'd been involved with the candy man, and the police process I underwent must have unsettled them even more.

After they raided the house, the girls all had physical examinations by the police for evidence. When the police took my brothers and I to Tracey's, I was traumatised. I was shouting that my dad would never touch anyone and Vivien just wanted to take everything from us. I was inconsolable. As a young girl without a mum, I loved my dad.

Vivien told me my dad was sick, that she still loved him but he needed help. She was going to stick by him.

Tracey, as far as she knows, told me that Vivien was fully aware of the way Dad abused her daughters, but ignored it. She hadn't wanted to call the police. It was only when Tracey found out about it that she gave Vivien an ultimatum. It led to her reporting Dad.

Dad eventually admitted his guilt to save the girls from going to court. Really big of you, Dad!

Dad was on remand in Basildon and went on to serve his sentence in Wormwood Scrubs. One day he escaped, and came to hide with his mate Billy in our loft. We all knew about it.

The police came and did a swoop on our house. It didn't take them long to find Dad and Billy in the loft. They both came out laughing, like it was some kind of joke to be caught for escaping from remand, where you were doing time for abusing your children. Some joke, Dad.

After that it was just us and Vivien, and without my dad around, the abuse and the taunting got worse.

Was Vivien getting back at us for what Dad did to her girls? I don't know.

I got a card from my dad after Mum got custody of us several years later. I think he's sorry but that doesn't make things right.

People have asked me why we have never gone to the police about Vivien... to be truthful we just wanted to forget about our past. We have all been so caught up with our own pain and emotions that we have never really discussed it in detail. Never discussed our unhappy childhood, our struggles through our teens, our struggle with holding down meaningful and trusting relationships, our struggle with bringing up our children.

It is not until I started putting this book together that we realised how badly neglected and abused we had been.

It has crossed our minds to take further action but what would it achieve?

We feel we will have a much bigger impact by getting our story out there. To bring the subject of abuse from behind closed doors out into the open to show the devastating affect it can have on children decades down the line.

More importantly to show that if the 'cycle' is not broken, the damage continues for generations. Often if abuse is in the family, it has happened in the generation before; there is evidence that this happened in our family.

At some stage enough is enough, the abuse needs to be identified, talked about and STOPPED.

Abuse of any kind is destructive, soul destroying and wrong.

My siblings and I have talked this through on many occasions and feel it is our duty to bring our experiences out in the open so that others in our situation can get the help that they need.

I AM OFTEN SILENT WHEN I AM SCREAMING INSIDE

School

I was too young to know if we were 'earmarked' by the school for special treatment. All I know is that we'd often get extra dinner, and once a year we'd get taken to the school uniform shop with someone official to get a new uniform and new shoes.

We were so scruffy and smelly. We had no elastic in our knickers so they used to keep falling down. Our shoes had so many holes in them that we had to cover the holes and keep them together with newspaper. We were called names all the time. Yes, it used to hurt but after a while you became used to it and carried on. That was life!

I did have friends. I made friends with twin girls called Sarah and Louise. We were all about ten or eleven and we're still friends now. They were new to the school so we stuck together. I often went back to their house for tea; their mum Jo understood. I was really sad when I found out she'd died some years ago.

When I was allowed out, I used to go and hang out with them. Their dad was a bit scary, definitely the boss of the house. I only went when their dad wasn't there - I didn't like to be around him. Their dad frightened me, but then most men did.

I told my friends Sarah and Louise about what was going on. I told their mum too. They got it. They didn't ask questions but they were there for me.

School was a lonely time for me, especially senior school. It was a five mile bus trip each way to Ravensbourne Girls School. I was bullied on the bus and didn't have many friends. I used to spend most of my time in the library, but I still loved secondary school - it was a sanctuary.

I think they must have seen something in me or I must have done well in my 11-plus exam because I was put in the top form. I was in the lowest sets in the form but it meant I was surrounded by good girls, which I'm sure rubbed off on me.

I always found maths difficult but loved English. I loved writing essays. I loved books, and because I didn't have many at home, I'd spend ages in the library. I loved fables and fairy tales: stories like *Jack and the Beanstalk* or Enid Blyton. I could completely escape in a book. The pages took me away from all the real stuff and they always had a happy ending.

During the holidays, we used to do some work for the local National Children's Home in Chislehurst, organised by Alan and Tracey.

We'd see the kids at the home being looked after and we were jealous. Vivien used to threaten us with the orphanage, but she'd say that if we went to live in the orphanage, we'd never get to live with our mum.

We used to spend all day weeding the flower beds. It was back-breaking work but we used to get invited to some of the functions in the home. I acquired a fake fur coat from the home. It had a hood and it used to come down to my knees.

I can remember distancing myself from everyone whenever I could. I would stand by a wall, wrapped up in my hooded fake fur coat, but I was cold through to my bones. Even when it was warm, I was always cold.

Vivien would ridicule me and try to take the coat off me but I would crouch down with my back against the wall, trying to make myself as small as possible, with the fake fur coat hood pulled down over my eyes. Trying to hide. Trying to keep warm. The more people told me to stand up and take my coat off, the more I ignored them and crouched lower, protecting myself.

The carers at the home would ask if I was okay. I always said I was fine. There was no point in saying anything else.

Once Vivien tried to take the coat off me but I wanted to be on my own silence. I didn't want to be in groups. I just wanted to be wrapped up in my coat and left alone.

Even now I get cold easily. I always feel that chill to my bones. In the main I like to wear baggy clothes and keep warm. At night I often cover myself completely, right up to my nose!

This year, however, I have pushed myself out of my comfort zone completely.

As a result of putting pen to paper, I have come to realise that I have changed. I have grown mentally and emotionally.

I had the opportunity to join a group of women to try on Nigella's wiggle dress and have a full make over.

For the first time I had my hair done, full make-up done. I put on a tight dress and wore high heels.

Even though people told me I looked fantastic I didn't feel this way.

This picture went out in the *Daily Mail* newspaper on 2nd February 2013 and *Woman* magazine in March 2013.

I have it as my Facebook and Twitter icon to remind myself how far I have come, and maybe, one day I will feel like the person everyone has described me as.

Since that picture I have been sabotaging myself.....need to figure out why!

Back with Mum

It was my brother Dave who eventually found our mum. Dave never gave up on the thought of finding her again, of getting us all out of the hell that was life with Vivien.

Dave had no idea where to start looking - no address or contact details. This was the 1980s; it wasn't easy but we were desperate. Dave scoured the streets of Penge trying to find her. I've no idea how long he looked for, or how many times he tried, but eventually he struck lucky and found my nan.

We set up a meeting with Nan in McDonald's. We were used to hanging around McDonald's, scratching around for leftover chips and milkshakes or scrounging for old burgers; but here I was - actually in McDonald's. I remember looking around the place with all the massive pictures of Ronald McDonald on the walls and thinking I'd landed in some kind of heaven.

I had a hamburger Happy Meal. Paid for.

Nan told us that Mum wanted us back. I remember before Wales how we used to see her, but after our midnight flit to escape the authorities, Mum lost track of where we were. She'd turned up on our doorstep but had no idea where we'd gone. Vivien didn't tell her.

It turned out Mum wasn't living far away. She'd got together with a new man, Fred, and had an 18-month-old baby girl.

We hadn't seen her for around two years but Nan told us Mum wanted us back. She'd never stopped looking for us or forgotten about us but hadn't known where to start.

We set up a meeting with Mum. We met in an alleyway next to the Odeon Cinema in Bromley so no one would see us.

I can't begin to describe what it felt like to see her. My mum. After all that longing, neglect, uncertainty and bullying, it was a lifeline. Suddenly we hadn't been forgotten. Suddenly someone wanted us, and not just anyone: Mum. She was the only grown-up I trusted. We'd had enough. We wanted out, and to find out we had a little sister too was just amazing. I remember clearly grinning from ear to ear and having a warm fuzzy feeling inside of me.

It's funny looking back. For all my mum's faults, I think her hands were tied. I could never leave my children and I don't know how she did but I sort of get it. These days if you were in trouble, with kids, there's always somewhere to go, but maybe there wasn't then. I know she wasn't in a position to look after us all. She wasn't working, she couldn't live with my dad anymore in the family home; she had to get away. It was probably us that kept her there that long. All I know is that I could never do it, but then I've never been beaten up by my husband.

I still have some kind of relationship with Mum. Most of my siblings have their own issues with her so have cut ties. I respect that completely.

I can see my mum is not the same person that she was 20 years ago. When mum was 44, she had brain and neck aneurysms which caused her to have two strokes. She is not all there mentally or emotionally. It hurts to know I can never go back. I can never ask her the big questions or blame anyone.

Am I angry with her? Yes and no. I'm angry with what happened but I can't be angry at her. If she was 100% in her right mind, I might be angry but I've had to accept she's not the same person anymore, there's no one to be angry with. She knows things have happened but she's lost the emotional attachment. The memories haven't a hold on her anymore.

I've asked her recently about what happened that day when I was seven. I can tell it's still painful for her somewhere. I found out that Dad had been having affairs for years. He'd also been knocking my mum around. I found out she'd took me with her. She'd had me for 10 days until I begged to be returned to my siblings.

It's funny but I don't remember it like that. I have a vague memory of sleeping in a unfamiliar house, with my nan. I slept on the sofa. There was a lady there, a man, and a little toddler named Robert. Robert was frequently beaten by the lady. She screamed and shouted at him continuously. This saddened me, made me cry, and I remember thinking, "I know what you are going through boy - be strong." I'm fairly sure this was during those 10 days when my mum went to live with Nan. Apparently I'd cried so much for my little sister Diane, she had to take me back.

After first meeting, we started seeing my mum occasionally. We'd get the bus to see her and stay for the weekend. She'd make sure we ate well and would buy us new clothes from the charity shop that didn't smell and weren't full of holes.

The first few times she did this, Vivien took the clothes off us as soon as we got home, as well as everything else we'd been given. She'd give it to her children. So Mum got wise and would change us back into our old clothes before we left.

Leaving Mum was unbearable. Every time we had to leave, we'd become anxious. Crying. Screaming. Begging to stay, but we had to go.

Vivien would try to stop us going to Mum's too. She'd threaten us, saying stuff like, "If you don't do this, you won't go." There was always a chore or an errand to stop us from going and a few times, it worked. Although towards the end, when Mum was close to getting us back, we'd just leave. Permission or not.

Mum's new man, who would become our stepdad, was very supportive of her getting us back. I think he's a complete and utter arsehole but I can't deny him the fact he helped Mum rescue us.

During the time Mum was trying to get us back, Vivien got worse. I don't know if Dad was under her thumb but no one stuck up for us. If we did anything wrong, her kids would snitch and we'd get in trouble. Of course, they were always making stuff up, but if they did anything and we told Dad, we just got told that we were one big family now so to stop whining. Dad never hit us but then he never stopped her either. Vivien would line us all up in a row and hit us one by one with a cane or whatever she could lay her hands on. All her kids watched.

I don't know why she was so spiteful. All I know is we were a complete inconvenience for her, something she had to deal with to get her money.

The hatred and violence escalated when Dad was in prison. Maybe she was getting revenge for what Dad had done to her kids. I just don't know. The day Mum got custody of us, we all just knew. We came home from school and Vivien was standing there, defeated. We could tell before she even opened her mouth. On previous occasions, she could not wait to tell us that Mum had failed to get custody.

"Thankfully, I'm going to get rid of you brats for good now," Vivien said.

We were ecstatic!

"It's important to talk about it. You raise awareness. But you also prevent it [child abuse] by not letting it be a secret."

Chris Witty,
American Olympic speed skater,
racing cyclist,
and victim of child abuse

Mum and Nan

We were happy being back with Mum. Happy to be out of Vivien's hellhole. It felt like at last we had some stability, someone we trusted, and someone who loved us and would care for us.

Money was tight when we moved back in. She had eight mouths to feed and no job but we never went without food.

Every weekend we'd go market shopping. It took us all day to get our groceries. We'd start with vegetables from the market (we rarely had fruit, it was too expensive), then on to the butchers for cheap cuts of meat, then we'd head to Superdrug to get all the house and toilet stuff.

We would get through five pounds of potatoes every night for tea so there were a lot of potatoes to buy! We ate lots of mince and lots of chips. We'd get through heaps of vegetables too. Cheap stuff like cabbage and curly kale.

I remember on Maple Road there was a shop that sold nice dresses and you could pay for them on tick. We used to put a certain amount down each week on stuff. My nan bought me a dress from there once. It was a burgundy velvet dress with a lace collar, the nicest dress I'd ever had, although by the time we'd managed to pay it off, it was halfway up my bum and about three years too young for me!

Every Friday night, my mum would get herself a Chinese takeaway. I'd walk with her to the shop and as a treat, she'd buy me a house chow mein.

Once a week we would go to my nan's where we'd get a crust of bread and a bowl of Sugarpuffs to eat!

My nan was great but she had a chronic digestive problem. She'd open the door to you and as she walked away, she would always be farting. Long, low, farts, like a creaky ship's deck, and as she walked away she'd be cackling at the noise and at how funny it was. We used to call her Nanny Grunt!

Nan and Mum were close and often went shopping together or just spent time together.

We did our washing in the bath tub. Mum would put all the clothes in and we'd tread them up and down.

Nanny Grunt had a spin dryer. One of those machines that you load from the top. We often used her dryer to spin out our clothes. We would put the clothes in then put this plastic thing on top of the clothes which used to keep the clothes down and then shut the lid. Nan would then lift me on top of the spinner to keep it still. It often jumped around all over the place. I loved this job! Mum and Nan used to have a good gossip whilst I sat there happily being shaken from side to side!

Nan used to talk to me about the children she'd lost, the children she'd looked after and fostered. She told me of her love for Grandad who I'd never met, and how she never wanted anyone else after Grandad.

She was there for me.

She gave me cuddles and bought me things she couldn't really afford, like my velvet dress.

She spent time with me.

She laughed with me.

She gave me the crust of her loaf.

She gave me bowls of Sugarpuffs.

She let me play with her dolls.

She let me play with her musical porcelain doll that played *Raindrops Keep Fallin' on My Head* she promised me that I could have this when she died. I never got it. This has made me sad.

My nan was a nomad; she could never settle anywhere long. It seemed as soon as she moved into a place, she was looking to move on; but my nan was there for me and my siblings, especially Dave; her heart was in the right place and I wish she was still here to see us all come good.

I know my nan has her own story to tell; she had six children including my Mum. There was abuse in her family, but this is not my story to tell except maybe to highlight abuse running through families.

At some stage, the cycle has to be broken. My brothers and sisters have decided that our generation is going to "Break The Cycle" of Abuse, to give our kids the freedom to grow up as children should.

- to be loved

- to be safe

- to feel secure

- Have high self-esteem

- have high self-worth

- to be free from hunger

- to be free from insecurities

Breaking The Cycle

Survivors Of aBuse

Fred. My stepdad. The selfish one

Since we'd been gone, Mum had met and married another man. Fred. We never accepted him as our dad but I always respected how he'd supported Mum in trying to get us back. For all his faults, he was behind her, even though it meant adding four more children to those he had from a previous relationship, and the two he'd had with mum, our much loved half-sisters.

We would learn to be very afraid of Fred, my sister more than me.

Things at home started to get tough again. Mum and Fred would tell us to do chores and we'd rebel. The trouble was, we'd had so many years of Vivien telling us what to do when we were children that we'd had enough of it. So at every opportunity, we'd question their authority.

"We've done this all our lives," we'd say. "We just want to be kids."

Mum and Fred didn't know how to handle it. We were being rebellious, especially the boys. We were damaged kids. We just wanted to be loved, and with eight of us under one roof, tensions mounted and things started getting physical. We really needed family therapy/ counselling but at the time it was not readily available and I don't think anyone realised how devastating things had been for us.

I remember how Fred and Mum would hold the boys down. These were my brothers who I'd fought so hard to protect all those years with Vivien, and now my mum and Fred would be pinning them down and laying into them.

It wasn't just Fred. When Mum drank, she'd get handy with her fists too. I'd go into the kitchen and scream my head off. "STOP ATTACKING THEM," I'd shout, unable to articulate what was going on in my head. I couldn't handle it. All those years of being caned and punished by Vivien whilst Dad looked on came back to haunt me. All those years of holding it together, holding my little family together under Vivien's ugly, demeaning tyranny, and now, back in the safety of mum's home, my precious brothers were being beaten up for being boys.

Mum and Fred would tell me to get out but I'd just scream at them: "Who do you think you are? You shouldn't be doing what you're doing!" I knew it wasn't right but I couldn't get it out right. I'd just be a rush of confused, all-consuming adrenaline and stress.

Every time they got in trouble, they'd get beaten. It wasn't punishment, it was abuse. My mum used to hit my little brother Michael because he reminded her of his real dad. It reminded her of how she used to be treated. My real dad used to beat my mum up, so she took it out on Michael. Little Michael, who for all those years we had protected and held in the night, in his smelly, dirty sheets. I'd gone to school smelling of wee and got picked on for it, but it was worth it to protect Michael. All those years, he'd wet the bed because he was so afraid and so unloved.

How can you possibly pass all that pain and hurt onto a little boy? He was 18-months-old when she left him; of course he wet the bed. He was picked on by Vivien because he wet the bed, but he'd wet the bed because he was unsettled, upset and unloved. I tried to love him. I tried to be a mum to him. It's what grown-ups are supposed to do but I did it. Dave, Diane and me; we tried our best.

Vivien used to wipe his nose in his wee and smack him round the legs. She told him he was dirty and would have to sleep in his wet sheets. In the end he didn't own up to what he'd done because he knew what was coming.

Half the time, I couldn't protect everybody. I tried my hardest. I still try.

It really hurts . . .

. . . to think about those times when the adults had control and they wouldn't find out what was going on with us. We were hurting. We were hungry. We were angry. We just wanted to be cuddled and to be wanted.

We got punished for stuff that wasn't our fault. Not one of the adults responsible for us ever bothered to find out why we were doing all these things, they just punished us for it.

Yes, we lied and yes, we stole, but there were reasons why we did these things.

I dare anyone to judge the actions we had to take just to survive and to get on.

To try to get some love and some food in our bellies.

I was the eldest girl so I was responsible for looking after and bringing them up, but I was a kid. I couldn't protect them from the grown-ups. Grown-ups that should have been looking after us. That's what hurts. That's what has stuck.

The adults had control and they never bothered to find out why we rebelled. They just fucked us up a bit more with their fists.

Even to this day, I can't stand any violence. I can't stand watching people whacking other people. I can't smack my own kids. I think I have only ever tapped their hands. I find other ways to discipline them like confiscating their possessions for a period of time.

*

I think Fred must have felt overwhelmed; these kids were too much to handle.

We were kids. We tried the best we could.

But it was what he did to my sister that really made me hate him. Details of which are still coming to light today. Details which are too graphic to share. This book has opened up the flood gates in my sister's head which she says has helped her but now she is remembering the horrible details. Now is the time she needs to work though her feelings and emotions with professional help.

Her situation needs to be managed in the right manner so that she can grow from her traumas and not continue to self-sabotage.

Hide and seek

Between 1985 and 1990, I worked at our local Woolworths in Penge. I liked working there. Working was my way out. When I worked, I was independent, in control, earning money. Money which could pay for rent, which meant I didn't have to live at home.

It's been that way since I was 16, since the time I went to a local church group who were set up to help people like me get housing. In spite of the constant bullying, beating, neglect and abuse, they couldn't help.

They told me if I got pregnant, I'd get a council home straight away, but I didn't want that life. I wanted to learn. I had my heart set on a catering course; it was the one thing I knew I could do. They couldn't help with that either. So I took a job in my local Walkers off-licence during the week, Woolworths on a Saturday and during college holidays, and McDonald's on a Sunday. My jobs, along with a few government benefits, covered my rent on a filthy bedsit in Anerley Road.

At 16 I moved out of home, into my bedsit and started my catering course at Westminster College. Working and education was my way out of my hellhole of a family. Now it was just me, my bedsit, my bills, my boyfriend and my studies.

One hot Saturday afternoon, when I'd been out of that life for a good few months and was beginning to put everything behind me, I was chatting with my colleague Teresa when a familiar voice called my name.

It was a hot and sticky day. One of those days where all the customers were glistening with a layer of oil and sweat. It was that oppressive heat which made it feel like South London's smog was stuck to every inch of you, and it was busy in that store. A Saturday afternoon full of hot, cranky, shoppers who just wanted to get home.

"Chris, will you come over here please? I need to talk to you." Such a familiar voice. One I'd grown up with. It was my little sister, Diane. Diane was still at home with Mum and Fred. We'd been through all the same shit together. The same kickings, the same starvation, the same survival.

Diane had bought a friend with her for support.

We weren't close anymore. We'd shared a bedroom at my mum's house and Diane was the messiest person you've ever met. I was always really tidy so it used to annoy me. If I bought something new to wear, Diane had always worn it before me. When Andy came over, she'd just sit on the end of the bed with her arms folded just so she'd be in the way. I later found out that Diane was trying to stay out of Fred's way, that she felt safe around me.

At this time in my life, I was trying to put it all behind me but here she was. My little sister Diane, looking lost and totally petrified. My job was to protect her at all costs. That was the only way I'd ever known.

I instantly stopped my conversation and walked slowly over to Diane. We hadn't seen eye to eye in a long while. When it had all kicked off with our stepdad, Mum's second husband Fred, when we were becoming teenagers, I couldn't cope with her nicking things or going off at me anymore. We both had our way of dealing with all the shit that was going on and I'd chosen to get out.

Diane knew I disapproved of her bothering me at work and I knew her well enough to understand something must be up. When she looked up at me and I saw the terror on her little face, everything we'd fought over suddenly didn't matter. I saw fear. I saw guilt. My little sister needed me again.

"What I wrote in my diary is true," she said.

I couldn't get a word out. I knew what she was saying but my mind was trying to shut it out. Trying desperately to reject it all. It was easier to believe she was lying.

"Not again," I kept whispering in my head. "NOT AGAIN!"

My thoughts suddenly flashed back to the car bonnet and the sweets and the penis in the dingy bedsit.

"I don't want to know. I DON'T WANT ANYTHING TO DO WITH THIS," my head screamed again.

I'M TRYING TO GET AWAY FROM ALL THIS.

I searched Diane's eyes. If I looked long enough, surely I'd find she was lying. That would be better. It would be easier. I felt angry. I felt sick. I kept searching for something, anything in her eyes, and then I said, totally rationally, "I'm just going to see Mrs May. I'm taking you to the police station."

It was a short walk along the high street to the police station. I knew it was important to act immediately and I knew that if my sister had come to me, she was in trouble.

"What can I do for you?" someone asked.

"My sister has been molested by my stepdad," I responded. I was shocked but not surprised. Fred was a filthy bastard.

"Could you please take a seat and wait one moment?" he said. "I'll be straight back."

I turned to Diane. Even though she was 16, she looked like a skinny 12-year-old, which just made the whole thing worse.

Diane had always been small for her age. When she was six, she'd been taken to hospital to find out why she wasn't growing. She was there for six months. She'd looked more like a four-year-old than a six-year-old. Vivien told them it was because she was finicky with her food. She wasn't finicky, she was starved, we all were. Diane has struggled with food ever since she was little. Partly because of what happened at home and partly because of what Fred had done to her every time we'd played hide and seek in Crystal Palace Park.

It was a sweltering, hot summer's day. She was shivering.

After a few minutes, a police woman came in.

"Who's Diane?"

I pointed to my sister.

The police woman looked at Diane, "Who do you want to come with you?"

A little whisper croaked out, "My sister."

And just like that, I was back to being Mum to my sister and brothers again.

The police woman opened the door leading Diane and I into a small room. She sat us down and asked for our names and details.

"My name's Chris," I started, "I am 18 and I live on my own."

"Mine is Diane," my sister began, "I'm 16 and I live with my parents."

16. We were both still teenagers. Young people. But what we'd already been through together, it didn't feel like we were young anymore.

The sick feeling worsened as Diane explained to the PC what had happened. From time to time, the PC disappeared to confer with her colleague, leaving us alone.

"Why didn't you tell me this had been going on?" I asked her. I sounded irritated but underneath I was hurt that I'd shut her out and she hadn't been able to talk to me.

"I didn't think you'd believe me," she shrugged. "After all, we don't see eye to eye most of the time."

"Well, it would have been petty of me if I hadn't believed you," I snapped. "I know you've been a liar in the past but even you couldn't dredge up a story like this. Could you?" It didn't quite come out right. I sounded harsh but I didn't mean it.

I was angry. Angry that this was happening again. Angry that I suddenly had to be Mum again.

I wanted to believe her but all her life she had lied about stuff. Not about something like this though. She couldn't.

In that moment, we knew we stood together on this.

"We used to play hide and seek," she muttered through tears to the PC, "up the park."

I was holding Diane tight to my chest.

"When we hid, he used to pull me into the bushes with him."

Surely it couldn't be happening again.

Here I was in another police station going through another episode of abuse. This time with my little sister.

"The park was massive and it took the seeker ages to find anyone," she croaked. "He used to lie me down in the bushes. He would grab my hand and rub it up and down on his penis and with the other hand he'd rub my breast. Sometimes he'd go further and touch me down below. It was horrid. Horrid. HORRID." She was sobbing now.

I had tears streaming down my face too. Anger, revenge, disgust, building up inside me like it might erupt. At that moment, I could have killed the bastard.

HOW COULD HE?

Every Sunday when Mum had stayed at home to cook dinner, Fred would take us up to Crystal Palace Park and we would hide for hours in the woods.

My brothers and I would be counting and hunting for at least half an hour to find each other. It always seemed my sister Diane was hiding with Fred.

That's why when my sister came to me for help, that day in the store, I instantly believed her.

"I need your help," she'd whispered. "I don't know what to do." And at that moment, I knew that all those times he'd been hiding with her, he'd been abusing her in the bushes.

Even though my sister used to lie to me when we were growing up as teenagers, I knew she was telling the truth now.

My body just went cold. I froze. Another one I couldn't protect.

I remember those times it had happened. I'd try to find Fred and Diane. Something didn't feel right. I'd needed to find Diane.

"I'm fed up with this," I'd say. "Come out, come out."

They'd come out. Fred would be holding Diane's hand.

Even though I didn't know it then, when she told me I remembered what used to happen.

Diane was trembling. She started to scratch desperately at her arms like she always did. All of her anger and frustration was being taken out on her body. She thought it was her fault. She felt guilty. With time I'd learn that the scratching and self-harming was a way for Diane to show she was out of control and not able to talk about what was going on.

I grabbed hold of her hand and hugged her. Hugged her as tightly as my strength allowed. My eyes screwed up tightly as I frantically tried to make sense of the horror.

Not again.

Why us?

I knew that sick, guilty feeling too well.

*

Fred was taken in for questioning and Mum had to take our two younger half-sisters for internal examinations. We had to make sure that they hadn't been abused. The girls were nine and seven. The girls were put on the 'at risk' register. At least Fred now knew he was being monitored and I like to think this saved our half-sisters from anymore abuse.

Fred the Manipulator

When we lived at Tovil Close, Fred faked a heart attack. Fred always liked to be centre of attention. He'd been having an argument with us and he wasn't winning. So what did he do? He faked a heart attack.

I knew he was a prat. I knew he was a manipulative bastard.

He just clutched his chest and fell down on the floor.

Mum was shouting and screaming at me for causing the upset and yelling at me to call an ambulance but I knew he was faking it and I told them so.

Fred went to hospital but soon after discharged himself and walked home with nothing on his feet. There was nothing wrong with him all along.

David with me as a baby

David age three with me, age two

Me age two and a half

Michael, Diane, David, and me

After running the London Marathon 2010 in
4 hours 43 minutes with a bad hip

In 2012 after second hip op

Me today

"You feel vulnerable. You can't do anything. You are helpless."

Chris Tuck

Alcohol/Football/Sunday Dinners

Mum never had any spare money. Fred didn't work.

Occasionally he'd do work on the side to get cash in hand. He would demand money from Mum so he could go out for a drink on a daily basis. We were trying to make ends meet and often went without so he could go to the pub.

I hated football on Sundays. The noise. The chanting. I associated it with what went on when he got home from the pub.

While he was gone, Mum would be stressed. "We've got to get the dinner on the table," she'd fuss. "We've got to get it ready for when Fred comes home."

"Don't upset him," she'd order. "You know what he's like." But we all knew that whatever we did, said or cooked, it would end up the same way.

"Eat your dinner up. Behave yourself kids," she'd go on. "Be quiet. The quicker we can get through the food, the quicker we can all get on." The tension mounted. We'd all be on edge, knowing exactly how the afternoon would end up when he got home.

Fred never gave us a choice.

He'd come home from the pub and use absolutely any excuse to pick a fight.

He'd pick at something and tell us how rubbish we all were.

"I'm not eating this shit," he'd say through bloodshot eyes, all beer breath and frustration. "This is all shit."

Then he'd turn the dinner table upside down.

He'd put Mum down, shouting at her and belittling her into submission. He made us feel scared. He made us feel vulnerable.

We'd sit there shaking with fear, but behind the fear I remember the anger. I wanted to hit out and hit back but something stopped me from doing it. He controlled us.

When you're a kid . . . when you're small . . . they are bigger than you. You feel like if you create a scene, things are going to be worse for you. So you say nothing. We learnt this under Vivien's tyranny.

The adults have got the control. You feel vulnerable. You can't do anything. You are helpless. So you sit quietly with your fear and your anger and you console yourself with the thought that one day . . .

One day, mate, you are going to get it. I will get my revenge. One day, you had better watch out.

It killed me that my mum was taking it from him.

It killed me that my brothers' and sisters' lives were being made a misery.

We'd worked hard, slogged our guts out making his dinner.

When he was in this mood, there was no escape.

I'd often go to my room and listen to the charts on the radio. I'd dance away for hours. I'd exercise for two hours to block out everything that was happening. Come to think of it, this was my first real experience of music. We didn't have a television until we moved back in with Mum. I had no idea about television programmes, celebrities or music. Even when we lived with Mum and Fred, it was him who decided what we watched. It was those afternoons when I was escaping his drunken moods that I turned up my old fashioned radio and danced around my room.

If we could get out, we escaped the house as quickly as we could and stayed out of the adults' way. Dave and I would often go to Crystal Palace Park on our old rusty bikes and play in the adventure play park.

This is where I met my husband-to-be.

NEGLECTED CHILDREN ARE MADE TO FEEL INVISIBLE

Wham!

I t was around this time that I made friends with a girl called Michelle. We both lived on the Tovil estate in Penge and would hang out together as often as we could.

Michelle was into fashion and music, something I had very little previous exposure to. Life with Vivien had meant no luxuries like television, radio or even magazines. My only culture was books in the school library.

Michelle taught me all a teenage girl needed to know about fashion and music. At this time I was earning money from a paper round and all my money was spent on George Michael posters, (which adorned my half of the bedroom wall), magazines, badges and sweat bands.

I had an old record player that played vinyl singles and I can remember playing the few *Wham!* records that I owned over and over.

The first time I went to Michelle's house, she introduced me to all the old *Wham!* tracks. She'd play a song and she would often ask why I didn't know who sang it or when it had first been released. This was the first time I really understood how sheltered my childhood had been. I didn't even know about huge news stories that had happened between 1977 and 1983, I'd missed out on so much. More importantly, I'd missed out on the early days of *Wham!*.

We used to spend hours in her bedroom doing our hair with curling tongs, dancing and singing along to *Wham!* using our hairbrush microphones. Michelle also introduced me to make-up, although it wasn't a big success. It made my eyes itch so make-up and I didn't last long!

Michelle's family home was really relaxed. She could do what she wanted, when she wanted. She was given pocket money and never seemed to go without anything.

I wasn't jealous of her, I was just thankful I had a part in this little oasis whenever I could get away from home. Above all, I'm thankful to Michelle for getting me into music.

Since 1984, I have listened to all types of music from all different bands and genres, but my favourite is the music of the 1960s. It's uplifting and you can hear the words!

When I was 14, I met my Andy. I was playing in the adventure playground in Crystal Palace. I think he fancied my mate Michelle more because she had big boobs! I didn't ever have much confidence but knew there was something special about Andy.

I made a deal with my friend Michelle. I knew that my boyfriend fancied her more than me and that his mate Dave fancied me, but I wanted a boyfriend. So I made a deal with Michelle that I'd ask Andy out and she'd ask Dave out, then after a month we'd swap. I knew I would never swap. I'd learned how to be devious because it was the only way I'd survived. So when we hopped on the 227 bus from Crystal Palace one day, on the way to school, we whistled and shouted out, "Will you go out with us?" They shouted back, "Yeah, alright."

Andy and I have been together for 28 years. Married. Two children. He knows everything about my childhood: more or less.

He found out because of the day my stepdad, Fred, caught us kissing in my mum's kitchen. I was 14. He came in and caught us at it. I was sitting on the top counter having a kiss and a cuddle with Andy.

"Oi, you love birds. Stop doing that," he growled and then with a smirk said, "Chris, you're getting big tits." Before I knew it, he came up and he touched my boob. I don't know why he grabbed my boob but he did. He'd never touched me like that before.

Fred moved away laughing, saying something really derogatory.

I couldn't believe he'd done it. I pushed Andy out of the way and kneed Fred in the nuts. He was doubled over screaming. Mum came in screaming at me. I said if he ever touched me again like that, I'd kill him.

I meant it.

BRUISES FADE BUT THE PAIN LASTS FOREVER

Bullies

After a few months of going out with Andy, Michelle realised that I was never going to give him up. She spoke to a few of her friends about it and they started to bully me. Michelle was still my friend and didn't condone the bullying but she couldn't stop it.

Four girls used to follow me from the bus stop in Crystal Palace to our school in Bromley and back again. They would taunt me at school if they had the chance, but I was in different sets to them so it wasn't that often and when we were at school my friends always stuck up for me.

The bullies were Asian, black and white. They called me names and threw stones at me as they trailed me down the road to and from school. They would sit behind me on the bus, pulling my hair and jabbing me in the back. I was often in tears but I never let them see they had got to me. They were menacing and threatening and I was constantly watching my back.

I met and started going out with Andy, my husband, in 1984 when we were 14. We've now been married for 18 years and together for 28. The Asian girl, one of my bullies, thought that she should be going out with Andy and not me. She told me so!

Andy has Welsh ancestry in him which gives him a darker colouring. The Asian girl told me that he was her 'kind' and not mine and that I had no right in going out with him. So most of the bullying was to undermine me in Andy's eyes and cause me misery in the process.

I told the school and my mum I was being bullied but nothing was said or done about it. I told Andy what the Asian girl said to me and he laughed, told me not to worry. I must admit at the time I felt threatened. I felt like Andy would leave me for someone else because of my baggage and being poorer than most of our friends.

Then one day I just had enough. We were on the 227 bus, going to school from Crystal Palace when I saw red and lost it.

I was sitting on the second to last seat on the 227 bus, on the right hand side with my friend Michelle. Andy was sitting in the same seat with his mate Dave but on the left side of the bus, across the aisle.

The Asian girl and her cronies got on and sat behind us on the last seat that went right across the back of the bus. Immediately they started taunting me and pulling my hair in front of Andy. They'd never done this in front of him before.

My inner voice was saying to me:

"How much longer are you going to put up with this?

"She is showing you up in front of your boyfriend.

"You are weak!

"Why don't you stick up for yourself?"

I felt my mind go blank. I felt myself stand up, turn around to face the Asian girl and ask her to stop. She laughed in my face and one of her cronies pushed me. I got hold of the Asian girl, pushed her down onto the back seat and started to slam my fists into her face.

Pummel after pummel. I was shouting and screaming at her.

I can't remember what I was saying but I do remember a huge sense of relief wash over me.

I was sticking up for myself! Not just for the bullying, for EVERYTHING! Everything that I had suffered beforehand. The mental, the physical and the sexual abuse. Unfortunately this girl was getting the lot!

I'd been bullied at school, at home and on the streets. It had taken me a long time and a lot of pain before I took action, before I finally stood up for myself.

The pain and fear of having Andy taken away from me had tipped me over the edge. She was threatening my sanctuary. Andy had been my rock for so long and I wasn't about to have someone threaten me with the prospect of him being taken away.

She got it all.

I finally heard someone scream, "She is going to kill her." I came to my senses ... I was breathing really hard ... I asked her if she was sorry ... she said she was. I asked her if she would stop bullying me. She agreed.

Once she agreed, I let her get up. I was shaking all over. Adrenaline was coursing through my body! I felt fantastic, like I'd just had a massive thrill but at the same time I was disgusted with myself.

After this frenzied attack, people at school especially the 'bad' girls, came up to me and patted me on the back. They gave me respect. This made me uncomfortable. I was the centre of attention. I didn't like being the centre of attention, especially for the wrong reason.

I did not like the thought of being a violent person. It went against everything that I believed in because of my past. I had been through too much myself and I did not want to be a violent person. This was not me.

I knew from that day that I would have to watch my temper and channel my pent-up emotions into something else.

When I lived in my bedsit in Anerley Road, I started going to a local aerobics and circuits class. This made me feel brilliant and was a great release for me. I felt calmer, in control and happy. I suppose it was the first time I realised that exercise could help manage my emotions.

Moving out

I left home as soon as I could.

The continuous abuse with Mum and Fred made all of us leave home one at a time before or at the age of 16. Dave left first, followed by me, Diane, Mick, and eventually the younger two sisters.

I knew I needed to get away from it all. From free school dinner stamps to scrounging for money, I'd always known I would need emergency money for a time like this.

Since I was 15 I'd started storing things away for the day I'd move out. I devoted a cupboard in my bedroom to stashing away everything I'd need to set up on my own. I'd buy household items when they came into the sale at Woolworths to make my earnings go further.

Mum would say to us, "If you don't like the rules under my roof, you can leave."

Every time she said it, I thought about my cupboard and secretly smiled to myself. I knew it was just a matter of time. I had my own cups and saucers, a kettle, an iron and an ironing board.

As well as Woolworths, I got a Sunday job at our local McDonald's and an evening job in an off-licence.

Although I was only 15, I knew I needed to find a place to live. I had to furnish the place, pay for the place. I was not legally old enough to leave home but I was too old to go into a children's home.

I also knew I wanted to go onto further education.

It was at this point that I'd gone to the church housing association for help and guidance and reached a dead end. I wanted kids but now wasn't the time. I needed and wanted a stable and secure environment before I had my children.

I'd already made up my mind that stability meant marriage, a good income and a permanent roof over my head.

Once I'd made this decision, there was no going back. I knew I had to get to college but I didn't know how I would afford it. I knew I had to get a place to live but I had no idea where to start looking. For both education and housing, I needed money but if I was going into full-time education, how could I earn enough?

These were my challenges but I also knew that the alternative, doing nothing, was not an option! The pain of doing nothing and staying with Mum and Fred far outweighed what seemed to be the insurmountable challenges of leading an independent life of my own.

In spite of these challenges, making these decisions and knowing there was no alternative meant life started to change for me. It was on my terms. I'd fully committed to my decision and although I found it difficult to accept help, people did start coming to my aid at the right time.

Like Mr Walker, who owned our local off-licence. He pretty much got me my first job and my first home. Just before my sixteenth birthday I moved into a grotty bedsit, paid for in part by benefits but mainly through my part-time and holiday work. Mr Walker had lots of bedsits. My one was £110 per month.

Then my friend Arwen's mum explained to me I could apply for a grant to help fund my catering course. She helped me get the forms and helped me fill out the application.

Committing to a decision and learning to accept help have been the two biggest factors in my life that have enabled me to knock down massive brick walls. The decisions I made at 15 were pivotal in turning my life around.

Learning to accept help has always been an issue for me. An abused child learns not to ask for help but to survive. An abused child cannot trust adults, but my reasons for change were so great that at this point in my life I had to accept help.

I couldn't just take help though, I had to repay it and I still do. I never want to feel like I owe anyone anything. Even now, I won't ask for help despite needing it. I have to have the time or the money to repay what I see as a debt. I only ask if I know I have helped the person in return in some way.

*

So at 16 I started my catering course at Westminster College. It was tough juggling all the bills but at last I felt I was escaping and making something of myself. It was a way out. In my mind if I studied and got a good job, I'd be alright - but a childhood full of disorder and abuse started to reveal itself in other ways. The memories would just keep coming to get me.

One evening I was working at Walkers, the off-licence. Walkers was a long shop where you came in at the front and went out at the front. You had to walk around the whole shop in a 'U' shape to get to the till.

Another girl, Jane, was working on the till at the front of the shop. I was working on the deli counter at the back.

Jane had been getting on my nerves. She was flirty and had been after Andy for a very long time. My boyfriend Andy was our supervisor. The layout of the shop meant the supervisor had to spend most of the time at the front of the shop where the till was to protect the cashier. Jane used this to her advantage.

Occasionally Andy would come and chat with me to make sure I was alright. As soon as he left the front of the shop, Jane would call him back. She didn't like him coming to me, often reminding him that the supervisor should be at the front.

This grated on me! I don't like playing games. Andy was my boyfriend and I didn't take it lightly that Jane was trying to poach him. Andy couldn't see what she was doing and when I spoke to him about it, he told me to lighten up!

This is how this particular evening was panning out. I was unhappy with Jane's constant flirting and getting angry and stressed that Andy wasn't listening to me.

I was wiping down the meat machine on the deli counter after serving a customer when I looked up and saw my dad and Vivien. I just stood rooted to the spot. I hadn't seen Dad for at least five years, since the day he blanked me outside Woolworths in Penge after he'd been released from prison.

I didn't say a word. They didn't say a word! They just looked at me and I at them.

They carried on walking towards the front of the shop. I was in disbelief and thought I must be making it up. There was no reason for them to be there, in that particular shop I worked in.

Time stood still. I was shaking. I called Andy down. He was nearly to me when Jane called him back.

I lost my temper and told him I needed to talk to him right away. Andy saw what state I was in and came and gave me a hug. He asked me what was wrong and I told him about Vivien and my dad coming in.

Before we knew it, there they were again. Looking at me, but not saying anything. It was almost like they were making sure it was me. Why?

They left the shop and Andy and I followed after them. We exited the shop as they were getting into a car on Anerley Road. As Dad got into the car, he waved to me.

I just stood there, dumbfounded. Why come and seek me out? What was the point?

It just did not make sense to me. For a long time I was left wondering, why?

I am 43 now and I have not seen my dad since that day.

I've had time to reflect on how I feel about him now. It's sad but I do have some happy memories - of times before Vivien and before the sexual abuse.

I remember running alongside my dad as he strode down the road, holding his hand.

I remember sitting on the back of his bike in a child's seat. He would often take me to work with him. I was really proud to go to work with him, with my dad, the carpenter.

I remember he used to make me laugh and annoy me when he used to rub his beard and stubble against my face.

I remember him picking me up off the ground when I was sobbing for Mum to come back and carrying me inside.

I remember him always lying down on the sofa with his nose in a book. I think I take after him in this respect. I love reading books.

I remember his love of tropical and cold water fish. We had stunning tanks in our house at Jasmine Grove.

We had the best Christmas ever in 1977.

I remember him giving us 50p to go and buy penny sweets on a Saturday morning for all of us.

I remember him trying to teach me maths in Wales on top of the hill.

I remember him driving the blue van in Wales, telling me he was going to take us four and leave Vivien, but at that moment the van's radiator blew and we were not going anywhere.

I remember the fantastic water fights we used to have in Stanley Road.

I remember the red bracelet that he bought for me on his day release from prison. This is still in my jewellery box to this day.

I have the birthday card he sent to me for my eleventh birthday telling me he loved me and Diane, and to be a good girl for my mum.

I remember him searching me out in Walkers off-licence, but I don't know why.

I also remember him rejecting me in favour of my stepsisters. He just sat there with a resigned expression on his face telling me we all had to get along.

I remember him beating my brothers.

I remember him taking a back seat and letting Vivien get away with what she was doing.

I remember when he killed our pet rabbits and made us eat them.

I remember him blanking me in Penge High Street.

"Child abuse casts a shadow
the length of a lifetime."

Herbert Ward

Mum and me

After I left home I would visit once a week, to make sure everything was okay. I would often take my sisters and brothers out separately and ask how things really were at home. If I found out about anything untoward, I would sort it out and threaten to get outside help if things didn't change. I felt really guilty about leaving my siblings but I needed to get on with my own life. I needed to find my own feet.

Mum was often sporting new bruises when I arrived, or she'd just look really down in the dumps. When I found out what Fred was doing to her, I told her to leave him. I frequently offered to get her the help she needed. She always told me that things were okay, and it was her fault as much as his, and that she loved him!

It was a few years after I'd left that Mum had her aneurysms. After that she just wasn't the same person. Before her strokes, I could have had a conversation with her about everything that had gone on and maybe got a sensible answer, but now she seems to have forgotten a lot of what happened. Conveniently? I don't know.

Mum often asks me why my siblings don't have anything to do with her. At first I would try to brush it off, but one day I'd had enough and told her it was because of what she had done to them. I elaborated on some of the details. She said she was really sorry and wishes that she could make it up to them. I told her they weren't interested - it was too late.

I don't know why but I feel responsible for my mum! I think that if I keep in contact, one day she will say to me, "Chris, get me out of here, I have had enough! I am truly sorry for what I put you all through. I am truly sorry I have stuck by Fred over you all and I want to spend the rest of my life making amends."

My relationship with Mum today still confuses me. She doesn't deserve any of my time and effort, especially now I know how nasty she was to my brothers and sisters when I wasn't around. It turns out she was more of a perpetrator of the abuse than I first realised.

My mum was there for me. She rescued me from Dad and Vivien for 10 days until I begged to be returned because I missed Diane so much. Money was tight but she treated me to things on the quiet. She helped me get over heartbreak. She treated me to chow mein on a Friday night.

Towards the end, just before I left home, when Mum realised I was serious about moving out, she arranged it so that Fred was out down the pub allowing me to move my stuff to my bedsit without a massive struggle.

Going forward, I think I will still visit my mum twice a year, and when she passes I will go to her funeral, but I truly don't know how I will feel.

I will be sad at the loss of a proper mother and daughter relationship. I am already sad for this loss but it is what it is and I have to accept it and move on for my own sanity.

This year has been particularly hard for me to juggle my emotions around my mum.

I was trying to establish more of a relationship with her, but after hearing some more devastating news from Diane, that put an end to it. I went round there on Mother's Day , but felt I was doing Diane an injustice, so just knocked on the door and gave my mum her card. I sent her birthday card in the post last week because I am on holiday on her birthday.

I am planning on meeting up with my mum to have it out with her in a sensible and civil manner, but I am not ready yet.

However at the moment I am a bit 'lost' in my head, but it will sort itself out eventually and I am sure it will be turned into a blog post :O)

FROM EVERY WOUND, THERE
IS A SCAR, AND EVERY SCAR
TELLS A STORY,
A STORY THAT SAYS,
I HAVE SURVIVED!

College

As a teenager I was cold towards people. On reflection I was probably a bit of a loner. At college they called me the ice queen. I hardly smiled and my conversations came across as hard and uncaring. I was just serious about my reasons for being there. My life and survival depended on it. While all the other kids were busy drinking, socialising and enjoying themselves, I could only think about getting qualified, earning money and keeping my head above water. My reasons for going to college were so different to theirs.

I'd fought hard to get my place and was working hard to pay my bills. My focus was on saving money, not spending it, but I also don't think I knew how to enjoy myself. All I knew was study, work and bills. There was little time for socialising, and to be honest, I did not know how!

It wasn't something I learned as a child. It's something I'm working hard at now.

In spite of the huge defences I put up around myself, I made friends with three amazing women at college, Maureen, Kathleen and Allison, who took me under their wing and helped me.

I found it really hard to make male friends. I didn't trust them.

The first of these three women is Maureen. Maureen was really down to earth and friendly. I remember her background had some similarities to mine but without so much of the heartache. We hit it off straight away; she even dated my brother for a few years. I always wanted Maureen for a sister-in-law but that was not to be. Even then, my brother's issues got in the way of his relationships.

Kathleen and Allison had totally different backgrounds to me. At first I was overwhelmed by the way they spoke. They were posh and seemed to me to have a privileged lifestyle. To them, the way they lived was normal, but to me it seemed like a fairy tale life and it overwhelmed me. For a long time I felt they were out of my league but they were kind and respectful and always treated me fairly.

Going to their big houses and meeting their families made me feel uncomfortable. It was nothing to do with them, they always made me feel welcome. I, however, felt worthless and inferior.

Kathleen lived in a big, posh house in Chislehurst at the top of Leesons Hill. Kathleen had older parents and they all doted on one another. They were a really close family. It was always a reminder of how dysfunctional my family and upbringing was.

As I grew up and away from my childhood, the friendships I made and different people I met served to make me aware of just how loveless my own childhood had been and how we had lived in poverty. Sometimes it hurt. Sometimes it made me angry. Sometimes it made me feel that life was just unfair.

On one particular day, I'd got the train to see Kathleen. I'd got off at St Mary Cray as usual and was walking up the hill to visit Kathleen's family. I can remember feeling particularly happy that day and humming to myself as I walked along.

Past/Present/Future

I looked up in front of me at the big hill I had to climb. I was looking into the low sun coming up over the houses and suddenly I got a chill. My clarity and the chirpy humming in my brain stopped and was replaced by confusion. I saw a too familiar silhouette coming down the hill, towards me. In the time it took for my brain to figure out who it was, my emotions had already kicked in with warning signs. Everything was screaming danger and I actually felt a cold, nerve-like sensation in my spine.

I continued my march up the hill but by now my body was on full alert, my heart pounding, all senses alert and ready to pounce whilst I fixed my gaze on the figure coming down the hill.

As we got closer and I began to register who it was, 1001 thoughts were racing through my head, none of them made any sense.

Panic.

What was I going to do? Run. Cross the road. It was too late.

Anger.

How dare she be walking towards me. How dare she!

Fear.

Suddenly I was a vulnerable child again but then I remembered I was an adult now and able to protect myself.

Opportunity.

I now had the opportunity to exact revenge and to beat the living daylights out of her for everything she had done to us. I was going to demand from her the reasons why she had treated us so badly.

The vision of that woman I'd held for so long in my memory: big, straggly hair; uneven and broken teeth; smoke lines around her mouth; these thoughts were swirling around my head. I just wanted to get back at her for the four years of hell and a lifetime of memories she had inflicted on us, but then something else happened.

As we got closer towards each other, I noticed she was smaller than me. I noticed that her hair was tamer. I started to calm down. She felt less of a threat. I started to think, "I'm bigger than her, I'm stronger than her. What can she do to me now?!"

I thought back to the bully on the bus who I'd beaten up. I'd felt appalled after that. I still felt guilty. I didn't want that again, even for her.

So at that moment I decided that the best thing for me to do would be to be the bigger person. I would pretend that she had no hold over me. I was secure in what I'd achieved with my life. I was doing okay. I smiled at myself.

When we finally came head on to each other, I stood as tall as I could. I stopped walking, faced her and said, "Hello Vivien, long time no see."

"Hello, Chris," she said, smiling at me. "Yes, it has been. What are you doing here?" As she smiled, she revealed a set of perfectly white teeth!

I was gobsmacked. She seemed like a totally different person. She was no longer scary. Even though my body was shaking from head to toe, I had an overriding sense of triumph coursing through my body. By my sides, I was aware of my hands clenching and unclenching slowly but I was calm and sane.

I explained to her how I'd come from my college in London to visit a friend who lived at the top of the hill in a big, pink house (I was bragging).

When I asked what she was doing there and if she still lived with my dad, she explained that she and Dad now lived in a mobile home in Star Lane and that they were both well. I later found out that Star Lane was the start of a really dangerous estate in the area ... a pikey estate.

She asked after my brothers and sisters and I just said they were fine. I didn't want to give this woman anymore ammunition to inflict further hurt and she did not deserve to know any information.

The conversation was very stilted. I think she was wondering what I might do to her. She was very nervous and seemed on edge. Recognising her fear made me feel immensely powerful.

We said our goodbyes and I continued up the hill. I was standing tall with my head held high. I refused to turn around and look at her. I refused to continue to be her victim. God, it took all my effort not to turn around, not to batter this woman into the ground for all the wrong she'd done to four, defenceless children; but at the same time I felt my heart slow down and my posture soften. By the time I got to Kathleen's house, I was exhausted.

Kathleen immediately sensed something was wrong and I explained to her my encounter with Vivien. When Kathleen asked me how I was feeling about it, I explained that I felt confused, powerful but above all, tired. I sat there shaking, telling Kathleen that I couldn't believe I hadn't hit Vivien!

Every time I went to visit Kathleen after that day, I was on the lookout for Vivien and her family.

The third woman who helped me through my college days was Allison. Allison was from a well-to-do family, in fact she was the first person I knew who owned her own horse! To me, having grown up on a council estate, this was just so far removed from our life.

Allison would talk about how hard it was to keep her horse. She had to look after it before and after college and it cost a lot to look after. This was another world to me. My main worries were how to pay my rent and still have enough money to eat!

Even though our backgrounds were so very different, Allison went out of her way to make me feel comfortable.

I remember Allison inviting Kathleen and her boyfriend Jason, and Andy and I to spend the weekend with her. This was a huge deal for me, so much so that I nearly said no. I was worried about everything, about how I talked, how I came across, how I was dressed - everything!

In the end I felt so out of my depth and uncomfortable but also desperate not to offend Allison that I told her how I felt. Allison was appalled that I should think the way I did. She told me that even though they had money, they were down to earth and did not judge people. We both had a cry and a hug and I felt much better and really looked forward to going.

There was a long train journey to Allison's childhood home. It was in the leafy countryside, a massive house unlike anything I'd seen or been to before. I was so excited that I was going to be staying there.

Allison's parents and brother were fantastic and lovely people. They made us feel so welcome. There seemed to be so many rooms in Allison's house all big and nicely decorated. Us girls shared one room and the boys another. I can't remember everything from the weekend, just that we ate well and had a fun time.

I remember sitting down for meals at the table with correct, matching cutlery and an abundance of lovely things to eat with lots of laughter and banter. This was a revelation but alien to me. It made me feel a little uncomfortable knowing how I was at home and not knowing how I needed to act in a social situation outside of my comfort zone.

I'd never learned etiquette, just survival, so trying to figure out how I was supposed to behave outside of my comfort zone made me anxious. For years it made me not want to go anywhere new, it was easier that way, but Kathleen and Allison always invited me out and did their best to help me fit in and to feel relaxed. I'm so grateful for their support and for opening my eyes to new ways of life and to new experiences.

The two years I spent at college were special ones. After college we went our separate ways but stayed friends. Allison and I were bridesmaids at Kathleen's wedding and Kathleen and I went to Allison's wedding. To this day we stay in touch, although we don't see each other regularly.

Maureen and I became really close friends and have always felt comfortable in each other's company. She has always been there for me. She gave me a settee for my bedsit (which was how she came to meet my brother) and we'd often go out together: me, Andy, Maureen and my brother Dave.

Over the years, Maureen and I have been in each other's lives. We both got married in the Caribbean, three months apart, and her husband Barry did the catering at my wedding reception.

Although we are all in different parts of the country now with our own families and different lives, I know that any one of these girls would help me out in a heartbeat and I them. Between them, Maureen, Kathleen and Allison restored some faith in me that the world is not all bad and there was more to life than the one I'd experienced before I went to college.

They took me to pubs and restaurants, helped me find work and introduced me to their families. They gave me their friendship and support and never judged me and I'm so grateful to them for that.

My brick wall

I used to punish myself. A lot. We all did. Me, my sisters and brothers. It took us a long time, lots of reading and a lot of counselling to realise that none of the abuse was our fault.

From the age of 18 to 28, I worked full-time and studied in the evenings and at weekends to become qualified. My annual leave was spent in a classroom revising for my exams. All my earnings after bills went on my education. There was no spare cash for holidays and no time to take any holidays.

In my twenties and thirties, I always felt like I had to fight my corner. I always had to get my opinion across. I had to get to know someone really well before I shared anything about myself. I needed to trust that people wouldn't ridicule me and make fun of my life.

I carried the guilt of my violent, paedophile dad; my alcoholic, violent, paedophile stepdad. The humiliation of having no money and of never having the latest clothes and shoes.

I could never let go of how my mum had known about the abuse but did nothing to protect us. I felt betrayed and let down by all the adults in my life who were meant to support me and show me the way.

I had an inner strength of survival and making it.

For years I believed that I survived my childhood with no help from any adults so, when adults try to give me advice I push them away. I live by my own rules because this has served me well all my life.

More recently I've learned that the isolation I created for myself was a result of stress and of not being able to cope. I pushed myself into a corner and put up my defences so no one could see vulnerable Chris. If I break, who is going to help me?

When my son was a baby, I had a mini breakdown. I like to call it a blip! I just froze one day when I was changing his nappy. I suddenly realised I couldn't touch him to clean him. I had no idea if cleaning his little bits was child abuse or not. I had no sense of what was normal. So I went to see my GP. Sobbing. I asked him if it was normal to not want to touch my son's genitals. I asked him if touching my son's genitals meant I was abusing him. My GP said it was fine, that I wasn't abusing my baby and it is normal for victims of child abuse to feel like this. He referred me for counselling.

It was as if every time I tried to make something of my life, every time I started to make progress, my past would keep dragging me down. All the memories would come back to haunt me like my childhood was asking me, "Who do you think you are, trying to be happy?"

Then, when I was 30 in 2000, I felt as if I had finally made it.

I had qualified as a Chartered Management Accountant.

I had my dream job as a Financial Controller.

I was earning £30k a year and had a good bonus scheme in place.

I was married.

I had my son Ben, who was 18-months-old.

I had my house in West Wickham.

I had savings in the bank.

This is what I had always dreamed of, but I wasn't happy. Why was I so stressed?

There comes a time when anyone who has been abused hits rock bottom, their own brick wall, and I remember my rock bottom vividly. For me, I literally did hit a brick wall. I drove into one with my car.

It was an accident. I wasn't concentrating. My mind was busy with so much other stuff. It came after a series of breakdowns, but my emotional meltdown was a massive turning point for me.

At the time I was in charge of the day-to-day running of the accounts department at the firm I worked for, and that meant managing seven staff and the computer system, which was always crashing. I was also responsible for budgeting, forecasting, actuals, profit and loss accounts and balance sheets. I was also put in charge of implementing a new computer system along with two consultants who expected me to do all the work. It was far too much for two people, let alone me on my own.

My 18-month-old son Ben was in daytime nursery from 8am to 6pm and with the demands of my job, I was working longer and longer hours. I would often arrange for my sister to pick Ben up and look after him until 8pm. I would then drive six miles to pick Ben up, drive six miles home, spend some time with Ben, sort out the house, get dinner on and get everything ready for the next day.

My husband is a civil servant and at that time he worked shifts. At this time, his job always came before mine and help with Ben and the house was not forthcoming. This is not uncommon in most households.

I felt guilty about not having more time with Ben, I felt bad about not giving more time to my job, even though I felt I was doing too much anyway! I felt angry at my husband for not pulling his weight and being more supportive. I was angry and frustrated at myself for not seeming to be able to cope. This was what I'd wanted, this was what I'd strived for.

To be an independent woman. To be a professional. To be a success. To be equal to my husband. To be a mum.

To add to all this, I felt as if I was being backed into a corner by the directors in my firm.

The CEO, Finance Director and the Operations Director at the firm were all male. At this time they were trying to float the company on AIM and the figures weren't stacking up. The Operations Director was pressuring me to inflate the figures. I refused. It was morally and ethically wrong.

The Operations Director and the CEO were getting really angry with me and the Finance Director tried to force my hand by explaining I wouldn't get very far in the company if I didn't agree. I told him if he wanted to go along with their scheme, that he could do the figure work and put his name to it. I refused to play any part in it.

I had spent 10 long years getting qualified and they wanted me to put my head on the line.

I was in a real quandary. I didn't know what to do. I could do as I was told and lose my self-worth and potentially be struck off, or I could refuse and lose my job and financial security.

Eventually the pressure from work, home and not being with Ben became too much and one day at work, I lost it.

I was sitting in front of my computer, trying to meet a deadline. I'd had an argument with my husband about something, probably childcare. I'd also just been given another ultimatum from my directors. I looked at the spreadsheet I was working on and the numbers starting to jump out from the screen. It was like they were attacking me. "The numbers are coming after me," I screamed.

As I screamed and cried in the middle of the office, I thought I was going mad.

I was too exhausted to understand that there was just too much going on for me to cope with.

I'd hit rock bottom.

There it was again. The memories, the anger, the years of bullying.

After a lot of soul searching and angst, I eventually left this company for my own sanity and managed to get a job working as the business manager for the Priory Psychiatric Hospital. Even this process was not straight forward! It was a smaller department than the one I'd worked in before but for the most part I was happy. There was only one problem: I had been so stressed from working for my previous employer that my periods had stopped and I really wanted another baby.

I'd waited 10 years to have children. I'd wanted to make sure I'd got a house, a car, a good job, a decent qualification - security. I wanted to make sure my family had all those things we never had as children. I never wanted to go back there. Now I couldn't get pregnant and I couldn't cope at work. I wanted two children, not a fragmented family like the one I'd grown up in.

Stressed and distracted, it was at this point that I accidently drove my car into the nursery wall. I knew this was a sure sign of stress!

Hospital tests showed up endometriosis. I went for a laparoscopy and we discussed treatment plans.

I've always had this aura of being superwoman. I've had to. I have a fear of needing help or asking for help. I don't want people to see me as vulnerable. I've always been the strong one, for my brothers and sisters and for my own family.

When I broke down, I eventually told the hospital director about my childhood and she said to me, "Chris, just think about what you want out of life and go for it."

So that's what I've done and that's what I'm still doing.

I'm stubborn and fiercely independent. I know I can always rely on me but I can't always rely 100% on someone else. So when I am ill, like the time I had my breakdown and the time I had hip surgery, I feel really vulnerable and need to carry on, no matter what!

All my life, I feel like I have been the mother. At times I've enjoyed it and other times it has been a burden. It made me grow up really quickly and I have never really been a child.

I know now I've suffered from adrenal fatigue, things have been too much and I felt like I had no one to turn to.

Needing help makes me feel vulnerable. But when you literally hit a brick wall, you really do need help!

On the Friday when we saw the doctor, the test results showed I wasn't pregnant, but by the Monday I was. It took three sticks to convince me but I was. It was mind-boggling for me and for the specialist, but around eight months later, out popped Charley in 2003. My little miracle!

"I've learned that people will forget what you said and what you did, but people will never forget how you made them feel."

Maya Angelou

Eating disorders

I've also fallen prey to eating disorders.

I was a product of a low fat, calorie counting culture. I had grown up listening to media reports about the dangers of fat, and having attended a well known slimming club twice myself after the birth of both my children, I had believed that low fat and low calorie was the way to go. For me it was all about margarine and the slimming club's bread (which, if anyone is interested, tastes like poo). I ate low fat yogurts, margarine, pasta, lots of fruit and salad, but no veggies because I couldn't be bothered to cook them.

I suppose I've always had issues with food, mainly the lack of it! I now understand that my relationship with food is deeply rooted in childhood memories.

My stepdad had an allotment. He grew his own vegetables and he always ate butter. I really hated him and tried my best to disagree with everything he stood for, so I ate margarine and learned to dislike vegetables. When we lived with Vivien, there were no fruit or vegetables. When we lived with Mum, she used to cook any vegetables we had for so long that there was no nutritional value left in them!

When my stepdad turned violent and abusive, it was usually over the meal table. I learned to shovel my food down as quickly as possible, then get away, before our dinner ended up in a smashed pile on the floor. There's the constant memory of our Sunday dinner plates smashed all over the floor or against the wall. Soggy vegetables in a heap.

We also couldn't afford fruit. I grew up believing that people who bought fruit and vegetables in the supermarket were rich!

As a child, I was always hungry. It was constant. A deep rooted, tummy rumbling hunger that's impossible to describe. I remember constantly feeling sick from the hunger pains and often I would eat grass and weeds just to have something in my stomach.

I even ate dog food once, when we lived in Wales. I remember it was Pedigree Chum and it tasted quite nice, but then I felt guilty about the dog not getting his dinner!

For a time after I had my children, I was obsessed with losing a stone. I was 10 stone but I wanted to be nine. It was just something that had got into my head, perhaps a product of the, "Your ideal weight is ..." mantra that slimming clubs like you to buy into.

I went down to 17 points a day, the lowest you can do on the slimming club's plan, and I even cut out the one banana per day I was eating because the leader told me that this was the reason my weight loss had plateaued!

I used to make myself sick too. It was a way of controlling emotions which I felt were overwhelming me. Struggling every day to complete college work at the same time as earning enough money to keep my head above water was stressful. Making myself sick was a way of coping.

I was never in a binge to purge cycle, I could never waste that money on food only to throw it up again. If you've ever been forcibly starved like I have then you'll probably understand, but throwing up makes me feel better. It's not something I'm addicted to, I'm very conscious of what I'm doing and why I do it. I know I use it sometimes when everything gets on top of me, when I start to lose control of life or when my demons come back to haunt me.

Diane used to scratch her arms and the skin around her nails until they were red raw and bleeding.

David and Michael frequently used to get into fights. Michael has recently told me he took drugs when he was younger to help him cope.

We all had different ways of coping with the past and making sense of everything.

Having gone through so much myself, I believe that I have the experience and empathy to help other people in similar situations.

BEING ABLE TO SURVIVE IT DOESN'T MEAN IT WAS EVER OK

My life now

My recent life has been plagued by injury, pain and surgery. It's given me time to reflect as well as time to regroup and retrain. Perhaps this is why 2013 finds me ready to publish this book at the same time as I'm re-launching my business.

I'm a holistic fat loss and fitness coach. I've been in the fitness industry for nearly 10 years. Accountancy is still a part of me and my business but I don't do sitting down at a desk for hours on end on a daily basis like I used to.

I started my fitness career in 2003 when I was 33. My children were still young and I was working as an accountant at the Priory Psychiatric Hospital but it just wasn't working out for us.

Working full-time wasn't an option with a young family. Ben was five and Charley only four months. Long hours and stress weren't conducive to a well balanced home life. I'd learned this (to my cost) back in 2000 when I'd had the breakdown at work.

It was in 2003 when I started to realise the strain of my childhood was taking its toll on me. I'd gone through breakdowns and exhaustion, struggled with eating disorders and low self-esteem. I always felt like if I just had the house, the family, the job, I'd be okay, but I wasn't. I was deeply unhappy.

I approached the Priory about a change of hours and the company created the role of specialist accountant for me. It was a real turning point in my life and career. I knew at this point that I needed to do something different to get more purpose from my life and work. I also knew that the traumatic experiences of my childhood and the need to support my family meant I could never compromise on security and a stable income.

For me, having a home, enough money to provide for my family's needs and having enough cash in the bank to cover us should there be a sudden change of circumstances has always been non-negotiable. We had nothing growing up. I would never let that happen to my family. Although I wanted more time with my kids, it was equally important to maintain my income. A constant need for security and stability, just another hang up from my childhood.

I thought about my other options. I had always enjoyed fitness. It was a way of coping. I'd used it as an outlet for stress throughout my life. Even since early days, when I used to dance to the charts on the radio in my bedroom for hours every Sunday evening. I did it then to drown out the shouting and escape from the drunken violence that was my stepdad. Movement and music made me feel better.

I decided that the answer lay in finding a career that involved what I loved doing. Fitness. I researched everything and eventually signed myself up to a teaching exercise to music course, run by the YMCA. It cost £750, which felt like lots of money in 2003. It was tough finding childcare for the weekends so I could go off and do my training, especially since my husband was often working shifts as a civil servant. Somehow we managed it. Education had got me out of my previous life and it would again.

During my training, I was a stone overweight and not very confident. Getting up in front of people took me out of my comfort zone. One time when I went to teach a warm-up to the group on the course, I forgot everything I had planned and practised and just burst into tears in front of everyone. This to me was a sign of weakness and that I was a failure, but every time this happens in my life, something kicks in and I just don't quit.

Towards the end of my training, my maternity leave came to an end. I decided that with my new career still in its infancy, I would need the security of my part-time income. So I took up the accountancy role offered by the Priory. This added another complication to my already hectic life, but made me even more determined to get to the point where I would be able to let the accountancy go!

One day at work I had an inspirational idea: to provide the patients at the hospital with a physical education programme. I spoke to the clinical nursing manager, who agreed to support my proposal once my training was complete.

At this time, there wasn't much physical training going on, but I soon learned that to the patients I was much more than a fitness therapist. Often we'd just end up going for walks, so patients could get out of the confinement of the hospital. As a third party, who wasn't a therapist or nurse, patients could talk to me and get stuff off their chests. It felt good to be able to provide more than just an exercise class.

I had also set up my own fitness classes. This had been my original aim, but as I saw clients come and go with niggling aches and pains, injuries, health problems and stubborn fat they couldn't shift, I became frustrated.

Clients would ask for my advice but I didn't have the answers. I wanted to be able to advise clients on nutrition and to help prevent their aches and pains from happening in the first place. I wanted to have an impact on my own, my family's and my clients' health. So I started to ask more questions and I started to read. Lots!

At the same time I was suffering from a lot of pain in my hips and leg. I became very frustrated with my own body. I've seen orthopaedic consultants, physiotherapists, osteopaths, podiatrists and doctors. I've spent thousands trying to get to the root of the constant pain and throbbing in my left side.

The early years of my new fitness career were spent juggling my family, my own classes, my work at the Priory and near constant pain. All the time I was trying to build my business, I was reading and learning. I wanted to know how to make my clients better but it wasn't until after I ended up in surgery that I realised how nutrition could be so vital to my health too.

In April 2010, I was going to be 40. I wanted to mark the occasion by doing something special. I applied to do the 2010 London marathon, running for a charity. I started my training in October 2009, running three miles, 5Ks, 10Ks, half marathons and then longer runs. The longer runs were agony, and I couldn't walk for a few days afterwards. Even writing this is making me wince.

Did this stop me training? Stupidly, no! I was more determined than ever to get through as much training as my body would allow, not realising that I was putting my body through untold stress and exacerbating my symptoms.

In February 2010, I was referred to a consultant for my hip problems. He also advised me not to run the marathon, but after all my hours of training and the money I'd raised for charity, I didn't want to let anyone down. Especially not myself.

I ran the marathon in 4 hours 43 minutes with a dodgy hip and lots of pain.

Between April and August 2010, I became increasingly immobile and the pain became unbearable. I was still teaching fitness at the time and didn't believe in taking drugs for the pain. Instead I let the pain tell me when to stop and rest. Unfortunately I seem to have a high pain threshold so I just kept on going!

After X-rays and MRIs, I was told I had multiple bone spurs, a broken bone and osteoarthritis in my left hip joint and one bone spur on my right hip. I think the condition was triggered by extreme malnutrition as a child and made worse by the repetitive strain of teaching fitness classes. Needing fitness to channel my stress and an imbalance in my nutrition as I got older had added to my problems. I had two options: leave it and suffer the pain and deterioration; or have surgery, which would hopefully rectify the problem.

I was extremely frustrated with my own body. I felt like I had followed up every lead and seen everyone's recommended expert to sort out my own problems but I wasn't getting anywhere! So, I continued to read books and e-books on nutrition.

I'd completed a nutrition course through the YMCA and tried to implement calorie control techniques in my first fat loss club but it didn't work – I was puzzled! I'd always thought if you moved more and ate correctly, this would result in improved health and weight loss.

When I'd starved myself doing one of the popular slimming club's plan I'd questioned the system, where you could eat chocolate and drink alcohol so long as you stayed within your limits. It didn't sit right with me. **How was this healthy?**

Having grown up with the calorie counting thing in my head, it took a long time to come round to a different way of thinking. At the time I thought I knew best **but it didn't work and I couldn't understand why!**

As more clients failed to get the results they wanted, I started to realise that the calories in versus calories out method was a load of rubbish. I began to feel a fraud for trying to deliver it. I wanted to be able to provide a complete service. I wanted to be able to assess all the facets of health, from mindset and lifestyle to hormones, exercise and nutrition.

Until this point I'd been very focused on exercise only. I had gone from teaching high impact classes like aerobics to teaching more mind and body classes like Pilates. My own knowledge and skill set had been increasing since 2004, yet my own mobility had been deteriorating and I couldn't understand why.

I started to network with fitness leaders like Rachel Holmes, Jenni Clark and Dax Moy, who had very different nutrition protocols to the traditional low fat or starvation diets!

It has taken a long time for me to understand just how powerful the relationship between our past experiences and food can be. The work I've done with Dax, which explores the barriers that stop people from achieving their goals, has been fundamental to my progress.

The eating disorders; the abuse; the violence over the dinner table; the sweets and the sexual abuse; the starvation; the rabbits, in my head it has all centred around food **and was affecting my health.**

I wanted to be in the best shape possible for my surgery. The right nutrition could benefit me, especially pre and post surgery. I needed to find out more.

Jenni Clark was a massive help to me in sharing her nutritional information and I am indebted to her for getting me started on this whole journey.

I enrolled myself on a **boot camp** mentorship programme because I wanted to start something different for 2011: a boot camp with a difference. I'd include nutrition and exercise into a results-based boot camp business. I started this in July 2010 and intended to launch after my surgery in December.

In August 2010 I put myself through my own 28 day fat loss programme based on my C.L.E.A.N. Living principles and protocols.

At just over nine stone I wasn't looking to lose any weight but I really needed to improve my energy levels, sort out my digestion and just become healthier. At the end of October 2010, I also needed minor surgery on a rectal prolapse - again related to poor nutrition as well as childbirth.

At the end of the 28 days, I'd lost eight pounds and eight inches from my body. I was astounded, I had so much energy, I felt alive and my pain was manageable.

I realised that I needed to roll out my programme sooner than January to gather some social proof of real cases, not just me. So I held my first Fat Busters Boot Camp in October and the results were staggering! Finally I was helping clients to get the results they wanted. Since then I have been working on my C.L.E.A.N. Living Programme and it has developed for the better in so many ways. I am really proud of it.

I learned more about elimination diets with Dax Moy. This seemed to be the next logical step in my quest to understand more about the interaction between health, nutrition and exercise for both my own health and for my business. It blew me away, I felt like I was finally getting the answers I knew were there all along!

The information I learned got my brain ticking. My own health and that of my clients could really benefit from this stuff.

My hip operation was cancelled and rescheduled three times during December. I was devastated. I fell to pieces. I was very depressed over Christmas and the New Year.

I was mentally and physically exhausted and in pain, so much so that I needed to share how I was feeling. I made a video of my feelings at the time, even though I am embarrassed by it; it is a true reflection on how I was feeling.

My pain seemed to elevate with my poor mindset. I felt negative about everything and I had to force myself to eat well. I did eat more junk food than normal for me and it exacerbated my poor mood and pain. Deep down I knew I was sabotaging myself and that eating well was in the best interests of my healing and my mood.

My surgery finally took place on 5 January 2011, seven days before the launch of my boot camp. I was determined to be up and out of hospital by the weekend so that I could start my first boot camp and not let my clients or myself down.

I was under strict instructions not to exercise but was encouraged to be mobile. I didn't realise how major my surgery had been and I should have taken it easier. I thought that if I was able to do it, I should do it. Going back to normal would get me through the recovery.

I was no longer jumping up and down: I was resting on the sofa, using both crutches, using the mobility scooter to get out and not driving. I was getting up at 5.30am, three times a week, to teach boot camp, Pilates and my general fitness classes from a seated or standing position.

I rested on the sofa during the day but worked on the laptop. I've never been able to rest, so to me this was resting!

I now realise that I was running on adrenaline. I was stressing my body big time.

Whilst I recuperated I decided to look into how the body works and find out what caused my problem and how I could fix it. I remembered what Dax had said at his nutrition workshop and I booked myself onto training in February 2011. This was four weeks after my surgery.

What followed was mind-blowing information and my second 'aha' moment when I realised I should not have had my surgery! Every time Dax talked about the body's own healing powers, given the right nutrition and exercise, I would get upset because I could not believe what I had done to myself.

However I have since found out that the deterioration in my hip from osteoarthritis could not be reversed, it was too far gone. There was no cartilage to save and the fragmented bone had to be removed. If my condition has been detected earlier, I could have improved the health of my hip through nutrition and the right exercise.

Four months post op, the joint wasn't healing and I was referred for further surgery. I was devastated. I burst into tears and again was low in mood for about a week.

Julie, the coach I'd been seeing through Dax, was a rock to me throughout - there were many times when I would turn up to see her and I would just cry! With a few wise words, I got back on track and my experiences ultimately showed me where I wanted to go with my career and my business. I wanted to be a health coach and practise health as my religion! If I could help just one person going through an unnecessary procedure then I would be truly happy. I wanted to preach health through nutrition and corrective exercise.

Although I was not at full strength, I decided to embark on a year of education whilst I recuperated. I looked at what I needed to do, what courses I needed to go on, how much it was going to cost. Dax really fired me to learn more and become something I can be proud of, enjoy and find rewarding. So whilst I was 'healing', I was learning so much.

When I found out about my second operation, I just carried on with my plans to get me through.

During my second operation, the consultant had to replace both pins in my hip with ones double the previous length and inject a bone graft as well. I would need two weeks of complete bed rest and to wear a leg brace constantly. This drove me up the wall but I stuck with it! I'm not a very good patient!

My rehabilitation was exhausting. I used my mobility scooter for the first eight weeks, but after twelve weeks I was down to one crutch on short journeys and driving my car short distances. I was finally getting there.

The roundabouts I've gone through with my surgery, the pain I've endured and the long periods I've spent immobile have really got me down. However, they've given me time to study and to think; it triggered my desire to find out what food is really good for you. My decision to search out solutions to these challenges have not only led me to my dream career, but have also given me time to reflect on my childhood, my past and my reasons for coming to this point. I finally feel content.

There is so much I want to do, professionally and personally.

My beliefs and values are to help people in any way I can, from fat loss, fitness and fun, to de-stressing their lives and minds.

I have three main business dreams to accomplish:

1) To be West Wickham's leading Health Coach. I coach everyday people to live a fuller, happier and healthier life through the Kick Start Fat Loss™ Diet & Exercise programme. I've started working with local businesses and have been dubbed by my local media, "a health and fitness revolution".

2) With Mel Collie, we want to coach our online and one-to-one clients to transform their lives by sharing our skills and experiences with them by adopting the principles of the "Breaking The Cycle" C.L.E.A.N. Living Programme into their everyday life.

3) I would like *Through the eyes of a child* to be a bestseller because some of the proceeds from the book are going to be re-invested into Survivors Of aBuse.org to help people get the professional expertise they need to heal and move forwards with their lives.

It's really happening for me now. I've finally reached a point in my career where it's working, both for me and for my clients.

"Families should be about nurture, love and respect, not fear, bullying and blame."

Chris Tuck

Reflections

My childhood was the pits. Emotionally. Physically. We'll all be scarred for life, especially my brothers and sisters with all they went through. It was constant, that's what sticks out. I'm not sitting here writing a story about the time I was groomed and sexually abused by the candy man, or the years I've spent starving, neglected, spat on, caned and bullied. There was more than that, much more.

What really sticks out looking back, is that it's a vicious cycle and unless you can "Break The Cycle" you cannot move on.

I was sexually abused because I was neglected at home and therefore vulnerable. My mum walked out on my dad because he hit her. She then married a man who drank and knocked us about. She hit my brother because he reminded her of my dad, who used to hit her. I didn't trust any adults because I'd been abused but I needed help to turn my life around.

I'm writing this book because I think and I desperately hope that I'm starting to break the cycle. I got out - and so can anyone. The memories are there but I'm sticking my head out of the muddy waters and sharing them with you.

Since the beginning, I used education as a way of escaping the poverty of my upbringing. By educating myself I could earn enough money to provide a roof over my head, put food on the table and have enough savings in the bank to not worry about bills and to ensure I could pay everyone back. My hunger for learning was like the burning hunger I had growing up; it's what ultimately led me to accept help and to turn my life around. The hunger brought on from only a slice of bread and margarine on a Saturday. The hunger that made me and my brothers and sister and I beg on Bromley High Street. Hunger that occasionally, shamefully, led me to steal food.

For a long time, I blamed myself for everything. I felt guilty and at fault, especially when it came to not being able to protect my brothers and sisters. It wasn't until I read other autobiographies like Dave Pelzer's *A Child Called 'It'* that I realised most of the stuff that happened to us was outside our control and that we shouldn't punish ourselves anymore.

When we were sexually abused; had holey clothes; smelt; we were ashamed and felt dirty, we didn't feel worthy of love. This wasn't our fault. It wasn't until I'd read stories of other people with similar backgrounds, talked to other people who have been abused or to counsellors that I was able to put things into perspective and offload some of the guilty baggage I was carrying. Families should be about nurture, love and respect, not fear, bullying and blame.

Seeking out the truth behind the emotion and having an open mind to situations that I've found myself in has helped me look at my options, evaluate my situation, put things in place that were missing, and given me the confidence to make the final leap to make a change.

I've made mistakes but they are my mistakes and they have been stepping stones to eventually getting things right and moving forward.

When I've made a mistake I retreat back into myself, lick my wounds, evaluate why it didn't work and sometimes I don't come up with a definitive answer. All I know is that it didn't work but if I don't continue to try or find an alternative, then I am not helping myself. I have the following saying:

"Nothing changes; if nothing changes."

You can moan about things until the cows come home, but nothing will change. Sometimes it makes you feel better, but mostly negative talk lowers your self-esteem and is damaging.

Taking action, even if it does not go according to plan, empowers you. At least you have tried and this frees you up to try something else and not have any regrets.

If my story has spoken to you in any way, or you're desperate to change something in your life, then know that it takes time. It has taken me years to get this book written, first as scrappy notes, leading to interviews, memos and eventually the finished book.

Writing this book has led me to reconnect with my siblings. We've chatted at length about family members and experiences. I've learned so much about the abuse we suffered from their perspectives. I've learned things that have made it all so much messier. We're closer now. We've been able to talk frankly and openly about everything that went on and how it affects our lives now.

My brother Dave had to get help with his behaviour. He's working through it but it's not been easy. My younger siblings have either blocked it all out completely or only deal with what they can cope with at the time. They fear that getting further help or counselling will make everything worse by uprooting memories they've buried.

We all handle stuff differently. I tried to bury it for ages and writing this book has nearly broken me at times but I'm moving forwards and I am finding myself. I am less angry and more peaceful within myself. Nothing is going to change overnight but I want to change so will keep striving.

I've recently had to get help from a personal coach to help me deal with the struggles going in within myself. It has been hard looking at myself and seeing things I don't like but I think I am a better person for it.

One of the things I'm trying to change is being secretive and keeping things from Andy. This could be about anything that I know Andy would say no to! My nan used to do it, so did my mum all the time ... "Don't tell your dad," but then I grew up having to be devious because no one ever said yes!

Deep down I just need Andy's full support and encouragement. I want to hear that he is proud of me. I don't need to be told no or to feel negativity. I have had a lifetime's worth of this!

It takes time, perseverance and support to deal with an abusive childhood or just to make a change in your life. Here's a start, based on my experiences:

My top 10 Tips

1. First, you need to have enough discomfort to want to seek change.

2. Evaluate your problem. Identify what it is, the truth behind the issue.

3. Research your problem, where has it come from.

4. See what others in the same or similar situation to you have done or are doing.

5. Find your deep-rooted 'why' or reason to make the change, because it will help you succeed. It will help you through those dark times, tough times. It will make you commit to the change.

6. Have an open mind.

7. Be prepared for rejection or things not going to plan.

8. Constantly evaluate and adapt but keep the long term goal in your sights.

9. Take small, positive steps in the right direction to build up your confidence, maybe before you even take the jump.

10. Ultimately you need to take the step, take action to see your plan through, but as I said this does not happen overnight; it needs all the above steps to happen.

The last few years have been a complete roller coaster for me. Even though I haven't been at full physical health and at times I've not felt mentally strong, I've achieved so much and am finally on the way to becoming the person I want to be.

All I know is that I can do anything I put my mind to. There will be more sacrifices along the way but ultimately I just want to be happy. I believe that when I can help my family and my clients, I will be happy.

I've finally reached a place where I'm ready to relax and be happy. I can stop and spend time with my kids. I go on holidays. I've been able to accept help and it's changed my life.

Yes, it still hurts and no, I've not totally forgiven everyone yet. However I've finally realised my memories are my memories and that's okay. It probably didn't happen like I remember it, but I was a kid and that's exactly how I remember it.

I've been through tough times but here I am, 43, married with two beautiful kids, the beginnings of a fantastic business and a huge support network of clients and colleagues. These are my memories but they're not my future. I am learning to put down my burdens, to move on and make my own happy future.

Letters from my siblings: Dave, Diane & Mick

Writing my story has opened up a new way of communicating with my brothers and sisters. Before I started, it's fair to say that we didn't all get on, that there were grudges held and so much guilt. We've started talking. Lots.

The dialogue and honesty between us now has revealed a lot about what happened to us, the way it's affected our lives and our own families and how we, as a family, can move forwards from this.

Only my real dad was ever prosecuted for what he did, but I'm not prepared to stay quiet. That's how abusers get away with stuff.

So I've had to talk to my siblings. They were there. They can validate my story.

As I've said in my book, it's about my memories. What happened to me and how I remember it.

What follows is a series of accounts from each of my siblings as told to me, in their words.

Three of my five siblings have given me permission to use what follows. Like me, they want to help other people. My two youngest half-sisters have recently requested to stay anonymous and I have respected their decisions.

I really appreciate them sharing their stories because it shows their struggle and what they have had to do to overcome their barriers and it will help other people in similar situations.

My eldest brother, Dave (44)

Fred, the coward.

When we first moved in with Mum after I ran away to find her and Nan, I thought Fred was okay. It took a lot of guts for him to accept four other kids, as well as his two.

I tried my best to get on with him by going to the pub with him. I remember he bought us a snooker table. But the cracks soon starting appearing. He would always be off out, down the pub. When he came home, he started on Mum, and then us.

It was all starting again: the bullying and being put down. As you know, Chris, we had an argument and he kicked me in the face and broke my nose. I forgave him for Mum's sake. We were all living on tenterhooks again, listening for the key to turn in the door. We would say, "He's back." You girls would go to your rooms, and me and Mick would be waiting in ours. I used to hate the smell of drink and the laziness of the man. I think that's why I'm the way I am today.

I used to think it was okay to talk to my wife and kids the way I was treated by Fred and our mum.

Fred bullied our nan because she stood up to him and in the end moved away from Penge to be near me. He smashed my car up when I wouldn't come home when he wanted. He'd called Nan and threatened me, saying I needed to move my car. I think we had been out the night before. When I came over to Mum's, I looked at the damage he'd done; the tyres and the headlights all smashed up. I saw him looking from bathroom window, smirking. I went to Mum's door banging and shouting through the letterbox, telling the bastard to come out and face me like a big man. But he wouldn't. God, I wanted to smash him up that day. I rang the house and all Mum could say was, "You shouldn't have left it there." It was in the bloody car park. He got away with it because I let him off for Mum's sake. I can't help thinking, why do some of you still have anything to do with Mum and let her near your kids? She will never ever see me or my kids again.

At his 50th birthday party, he tried it on with my girlfriend by saying she had nice boobs, and he tried to cuddle her. When I confronted him about it, Mum came at with me with a carving knife in front of everybody. That night, I left home for good. There you go, Mum showed her true colours towards her children again. So to me, he's a liar, a two-faced coward and now I know he's also a paedophile. I would never trust him or her with my kids.

My childhood has affected me by not being able to have a close relationship with my siblings. It has affected me by thinking that I'm always right and what I say goes. I used to look at women who challenged me in my relationship with the girls as interfering old cows. I was always argumentative and had a bad temper. Also because I've never had a true father or mother, I've never learned relationship skills. I've always found it difficult to express myself to my own siblings and, most importantly, to my own children.

I say let Mum live in her own misery with him. She'll be lonely and she's never going to enjoy being a grandmother. I won't even attend her funeral, that's how much I pity her. I'm sorry if that upsets you but I've had enough listening about her. She's made her bed, she can lie in it.

When Nan died, I had no one to talk to and bottled a lot of things up over a few years. Nan had been my rock. I'd lived with her for a while and we'd been company for each other. Around my 40th birthday, it all started to come out.

I couldn't have my party until I was 41 because I wasn't living at home at the time. I was with my wife and children at the party but I had a social worker watching how I behaved around my kids because of the problems they were experiencing from me.

I felt like I couldn't be trusted because I was being watched all the time by social services. But I knew deep down that I wouldn't hurt a hair on their heads.

All these people only knew about me was from a distance and from what they'd read about me. To them, I was a ticking time bomb waiting to explode.

There were times when I was away from my family and my wife Angela, and I wanted to take my life. I didn't want be here anymore. I felt alone in this world. I couldn't talk to my siblings as we didn't have the relationship that we have now. I looked at other families and wondered how it could be that they all get on and stick up for each other. "Why don't we have that?" I thought. "What's gone wrong?"

So one night in my flat, I put a chair under my attic hatch and hung a rope from the rafters. Angela didn't want to be with me. She was confused and was being told that she had to put our children first. I just sat there staring down the hallway inching closer to the chair. I took a picture and texted it to Angela. I was being a coward, trying to get Angela to come running and give me a hug to tell me everything was going to be okay. But instead she rang me and told me not to be stupid. She said that I would always have her and the kids. But I felt such emptiness inside.

I had no brother or sisters around me to talk to. I cried and sat staring at the four walls. Then I must have fallen asleep.

The next morning, it was a new day. I decided I was going to prove everybody wrong. I just found some strength inside me.

Two people from the family division came to interview me and we started work at fixing me. After pouring my heart out to them, the weight that I'd carried for so long was lifting off my shoulders. They could not believe that I was sitting in front off them. Most people they came across in similar situations had ended up on drugs, sleeping rough or in a mental hospital. Knowing that I was doing okay by comparison perked me up. "I must be made of some good stuff," I thought. Anyway, they wondered why we had Luke and Sam for years with no problems then Alex and Rianna came along and my childhood reared its ugly head.

Angela had to have assessments as well. She was assessed as an adult with learning difficulties. She forgets quickly. I've got three children with ADHD and autism, and a little girl with global developmental delay. Wow! I just couldn't cope with the pressure. It was all too much but I loved them all. They are my family. So I needed to sort myself out to be able to cope.

First of all, I went on a course called *Changing Ways* for 30 weeks, looking at men's behaviour towards women. Everything I learned from this was about looking at my father and my stepfather Fred, and the way they behaved towards our mum. I learned that their behaviour was not acceptable. It had been all I knew. Then I went on a 12-week anger management course to look at how I could control my anger. I learned how to have discussions with Angela and I could leave the room or go for a walk before we got to that angry point when I lost control.

At this point, I felt we needed more help figuring out how Angela and I could deal with our children's disabilities. So I went online and found ADHD courses and *1-2-3 Magic* for autism. I had ticked all the boxes and social services were very happy with me. I felt good because I was showing them I could change.

But after being let home again, it was still hard to change. I was falling back into my old ways again: Shouting at Angela and the kids. Our eldest two didn't want me living with them. Poor Angela was being made to make a choice: me or the kids.

I moved out again and from a distance I could see what my kids were going through. It was like watching what me and my siblings had gone through, being let down all the time.

I was back in a room again on my own. I could only see my kids at weekends, supervised by social services. This was crap for me. Not being trusted. It was turning their lives upside down. I asked myself, "Do I walk away and have no contact with them ever again?" A voice came into my head, "Nooooooo you don't. Your mum and dad walked away from you. How do you feel about it?"

Well that was the second kick up the backside I needed. I went to Angela's mum and dad and told them I needed help and wanted to stop fighting. They got Angela to understand what was going on. We went through the courts again to fight for our kids. The judge and social services gave us a supervision order, which meant they had joint custody of our kids. This was the time to roll up our sleeves and fight for them.

Sitting in a family court fighting for my kids is what finally woke me up and made me turn my life around. I was shitting myself, with Angela looking at a judge expecting him to take our four kids away from us.

The answer is obvious when you write it down. I was copying all the stuff I'd experienced as a kid. It was like looking in the mirror and seeing your dad's reflection in your own.

I will always blame myself and I still have a cry when I'm on my own. We are not to blame. It is four adults who abused us, bullied and treated us like nobodies who are to blame. Sometimes I wish I had never been born. I wouldn't wish my childhood experiences on anybody.

We went to Relate marriage counselling for 10 sessions because Angela still had doubts about me in the back of her mind. It was about communicating with each other because she had closed up to me. I was still so angry with myself for letting my wife and children experience all this stuff.

I went to my doctors and they put me in touch with another counsellor who took me back to being a little boy, pulled my life apart and put it back together again. That's when I went looking for other family members who were involved in my childhood to see what they could tell me and fill in the gaps.

I wanted to find my real dad. I haven't seen him for 33 years. I wanted to know if he ever thought about us or was looking for us. I wanted to spill my anger at him for what he had done to us and the impact it was having on us. I wanted to hit him at first and make him feel some of my pain. I found him.

But like the coward he has always been, he didn't want to know. He was with a new woman and she was controlling him like Vi had done.

Our mum was always being controlled by Fred, so we had no one to protect us.

My little sister, Diane (41)

Don't give up writing your book, Chris! That's how abusers get away with stuff. Why let them win? I have not left my inner child, ever, and the book makes it all real for me. It's not going round and round in my head anymore.

I have so much anger and hatred towards them.

Reading the book has made me so angry. The past has stopped me living. Reading what you have written has made me realise that it was not my fault and, at the same time, I am not small anymore. I am not that child. We have suffered enough. It's time to be the adult that can't be hurt anymore.

My head and my heart have always been so full of pain, anger and a deep sadness for that little girl which I feel I still am.

I feel that I am not good enough, not intelligent enough, and not clean enough. I have always felt worthless, stupid, unlovable.

I don't want pity. I want answers as to why four adults were so cruel and nasty to abuse and discard me the way that they did.

They were supposed to love me so why would they do that to me?

It's easy not to think about it - it's less painful to believe it's not me.

I don't believe I deserve a nice home ... why? I feel dirty inside and out; I will never be clean.

Beer, beards, slippers, cubby holes, jam, Sunday dinners and rats from Anerley Road. I loathe them all.

I have always felt dirty, disgusted, contaminated, and unclean. I am mad at myself for allowing him to do it. I am ashamed and I feel guilty for letting him do it. I was nine when it started and twelve when it stopped, old enough to say NO.

I have always felt that a home, a husband and career were not for me.

I don't deserve them!

Mum didn't love me enough, she rejected me twice. When I was five, she left me at school for hours. She just forgot about me. On another occasion, Vivien came and picked me up and told me that Mum had left for good. So it just proves I wasn't good enough even for my own mother's love.

Look at your Charley. Just think, I was the same age.

Mum does not care. She caught him at it once at Anerley Road. She picked him over me, she picked him over you, Chris, and she picked him over all of us.

I just want to feel loved and worthy. I want my feelings of being dirty and contaminated, useless and unlovable to go.

These feelings are not visible but they are there in the background hammering in my head. The little girl has to go. I deserve better. They failed me!

But most unforgiveable is that I am failing myself by denying myself love and happiness. I am not giving my kids the happy and loving Mum that I know I am.

Chris, I want you to share what I've told you with our siblings. I want this to make us closer and understand that we've only got each other, the six of us. Fuck OUR parents and step-parents. I don't want to see or hear their names again. This is screwing with my mind. Please, if any good comes out of this, I hope it brings us all closer. I'm here for all of you but you guys have to be the same for me as well.

I have one awful painful memory that I relive every day. It makes me physically sick and mad.

I hate slippers, banging and screams. I have to walk away.

In Anerley Road, I saw Fred hitting Michael with a slipper, over and over for wetting the bed. He was six and I can still hear his screams. I had to watch Fred and Mum beating Mick up in his room.

I am sorry I didn't help, Mick.

Since having my youngest boy, I get flashbacks and have nightmares.

I can't deal with banging. It drives me insane.

I had to listen to Mum and Fred hitting him, and Mick had to hide wet sheets in the back garden. It still eats at me that I did nothing. I can still picture it.

My life was okay until I was five, I think. That all changed in 1975, one day my sister Chris was kept at home and I went to school. At home time, I waited and waited for Mum to collect me. After what seemed forever, a neighbour came to pick me up. When I got home, everyone was crying. My mum was gone. She had kept my sister, who was seven, at home to stay with my two-year-old brother.

Apparently Mum left because my dad beat her. He was a cruel, cheating drunk. Yet she planned it all and took me to school knowing that she was going. I never knew she had said goodbye. A part of me died that day my mum left; I felt she didn't love me anymore. Today, whenever I'm late for the school pick-up, the feeling of desolation and emptiness returns like a punch in the guts; it's an awful feeling. Of course, my son doesn't feel like that; he is still in the playground with the other kids waiting for their mums. Sometimes your heart rules your head. I know being five minutes late is okay, it won't affect Zach. But it affects me, it brings back all those strong feelings of abandonment and being unloved. This is how I am still affected by my past.

The neighbour who collected me from school was called Vivien. She had several daughters.

This evil cow still haunts my sleep today. Vivien had apparently had an affair with my Dad before Mum left. Vivien moved into 4 Jasmine Grove when Mum finally walked out; all of us the kids were made to sleep in Vivien's house. It was cold and dark and not secure. At the age of five, I had to take myself to bed; I was always scared. To this day, I like all the windows closed and always have a landing light on, just in case the bogeyman comes to get me.

My sister and I used to have our own room with our own beds and toys and clothes. Vivien took the whole lot; I never saw anything again. I do tend to go overboard with toys now. I never had another toy until I was back with my mum at the age of nine.

I still saw my mum at weekends for a while after she left; we all stayed at my nan's house but were returned each time to Dad and Vivien. Why couldn't Mum keep us at Nan's? I was let down again. She didn't love us enough; that's what I felt anyway. Even in these early days, Vivien was cruel and my parents did nothing.

Shortly after, we all moved to London Road to be under one roof but life wasn't any better. We were dirty, dishevelled and always hungry. The kids at school tormented and bullied us. The detrimental effect this has on me now is awful. I have huge problems doing things and I isolate myself. I don't even speak to the mums in the playground because I feel inadequate and out of place. I get the same panicky sick feelings of not being important, a speck of dirt on the floor. Now I know I'm not smelly and dirty, and the mums are nice and say hello, but I sometimes still feel like that little girl. I change my clothing constantly and always seek reassurance that I look okay. I become annoyed if I got a negative comment because I feel rejection, but when I get a positive comment I don't believe it either!

When I was a child I was told I was useless, dirty, and no good, and it's imprinted on my mind even now. After all, when all four parents are saying this to me over many years, how can they be wrong? I felt that people in the street could see the dirt and evil pouring out of me. I don't like crowds of people to this day. I am not a social person. The bullying at school and home, being abandoned and unloved has created huge problems for me. At this stage in my life, I was wetting the bed, and Vivien would march into my room, check my bed then hit me with a bamboo stick across the hands or bum.

I cannot stand swishing noises and I hate fingers being clicked. The noise and thought is enough to cause a distressing flashback. I don't like fingers in door jambs either, as this was used as a form of punishment once or twice.

One day, we all got into a van and scarpered to Wales. I don't know why. We lived in two tents.

All the kids slept in one tent on the hard ground with only coats to keep us warm. The adults were in the other tent; this was six months of hell.

I now sleep with the duvet wrapped around me on my front. I have to keep my hands warm.

We were still hungry and dirty. We had to steal food. I even once had a raw egg from the bin.

We used to get one meal a day. Every Tuesday, Vivien made mince and rice. Even today, I love it because it was filling. I relished the sensation of a full stomach and the food warmed me. I should have had blissful feeling every day, but it didn't happen.

We were abandoned by my dad and Vivien in the middle of winter; they had gone back to Bromley. Our stepsister's husband had to come from Bromley to Wales to get us. Yet again, I was abandoned, cold, dirty and hungry at the age of seven. I started to feel like I was no good and that everyone wanted to leave me because I was bad.

Sometimes as an adult I still feel like this. Even though I'm invited somewhere, I don't go because I feel that I am not really wanted. I feel awkward, inadequate and useless. All my life, I have been left behind.

When we returned from Wales to Bromley, life just continued in the same manner. Our mum had moved and we didn't know where she was. It was during this period of time that my dad was convicted of abuse. I can't remember dates and times but I was taken to the police station as well. I had an examination like the others. I cannot remember the details of the abuse; I was only six or seven. All I know is my own dad used to get into bed with my stepsisters and me.

My stepmother Vivien used to make me sit facing the wall for hours at a time, hitting me, berating me and cajoling me … What for? The sick bitch used to tell me I was a dirty liar and not good enough for my father to touch me, unlike her daughters who he abused. Her treatment towards me has had huge and far-reaching consequences; her actions destroyed me and devastated the rest of my childhood. It also blighted my adult life.

I have weird ways because of the bullying and abuse. I speak very quickly and stutter; sometimes people see this and comment but they don't understand this in itself makes me feel more stupid and incapable. So I give up or don't try. It's not laziness or that I can't be bothered. It's having no self-respect and being frightened of putting a foot wrong and then being punished.

Who looks at a child and thinks I would like to have sex with it? I am sorry, I just don't get it.

What the hell is wrong with these people?

What do they see that we don't?

What do they think in the process of an act?

Can't they see fear, pain and horror in that child's eyes?

Can't they see what they are doing?

Why can't they see it after they have been punished and in prison?

Why can't they see it after they have destroyed lives?

Then, after all of that, they can still carry on and on.

Abusing, using, hurting destroying.......

For what ... a bit of sexual gratification!

Dad is lucky I don't know where he is today......

I want to give him back some of what he gave me.

When Chris told me that she needed to change some names in this book, I was appalled. I was physically sick. Fred used to come to the hospital with Mum and behaved like a loving daddy and let me sit on his knee. When we went to Crystal Palace Park and hide, he always took me to hide. Chris always said I was his favourite; little did she know that he was abusing me!

Fred told me I would go back to Vivien if I said anything and that was normal because my real dad had done it. I was told I liked it; I was a dirty girl, a whore. I was a small nine-year-old girl.

I was already shell-shocked from Vivien and Dad.

Fred raped me once but for years I was made to have oral sex or use my hand. And he did the same to me. He would often have me in his bedroom when the others were downstairs.

Fred used objects as well as his fingers ... it was painful and degrading. When we were at Crystal Palace Park, he raped me; it only lasted a few minutes because Chris nearly caught him. She had had enough trying to find us, as we had been hiding for ages. She came looking for us; on that day, I was saved from prolonged abuse. He made me look at dirty magazines and porn. The fact I was that small and vulnerable is hard. I feel dirty even now.

When I found out that this book was being written, I wanted Chris to name and shame but I understand that she cannot. I carried my burden around with me for years. I could not tell anyone I didn't want to be returned to Vivien and Dad; I wanted just to be free of everything!! I used to scratch my arms to pieces, I wanted my abusers to leave me alone! One day it all got too much for me and I went and told Chris at work. We went to the police station and reported the abuse to the police and they did an investigation. Unfortunately it didn't go anywhere because they said it was his word against mine.

The physical, mental, emotional and sexual abuse has kept me paralysed for years; I have not been able to function properly, not been able to live my life to the full. I have struggled through the last two decades trying my best to bring up my two older children. I had bouts of what Chris says was clinical depression. I fed my children but I was not able to keep my environment clean. I didn't see any point. I was dirty so why look after myself? Why tidy up after myself?

I lost my home when I could not manage to deal with the bills and my everyday paperwork. I ended up being kicked out of a hostel for not keeping it clean. I was suicidal at this point and Chris could not understand what was going on. She told me to get myself together for my kids, keep my hostel room tidy, but I just couldn't. I used to run out of money and often go to Chris for money for food. We eat fast food because I could not bring myself to cook and clean. Chris had just given birth to Charley via c-section when I hit rock bottom. I don't remember much about this time other than that I was homeless due to my depression and not being able to cope. Charley was three weeks old, Chris was getting over a traumatic birth and should not have been driving but she came and moved me from the hostel I was being kicked out of to another. She took me to social services every day for a week. We sat there with Charley until they provided me with some sort of housing. They told us that I had intentionally made myself homeless because I didn't answer any of their letters about my rent arrears.

To tell you the truth, I was in my own little world. I was not able to deal with anything at this time, I didn't care, and I was in a bad way. Chris explained this to the social services. She even asked them to take my kids into temporary foster care so that I could get my head together. They asked if I had hit them or abused them. I said no; they said they couldn't help. We were gobsmacked.

Chris was at her wit's end, she did not know what to do, so eventually after sitting around all day every day, we managed to find a landlord who would take DSS tenants. The social services used a fund to lend me the deposit and I was finally homed. A new start? Not really. I put on a brave face to Chris and promised that I would keep the house in tip-top condition but soon the memories, the feeling, the emotions, got the better of me and I went back to my old ways. Chris would visit once per week and call everyday to check up on me, give me a kick up the bum. Every three months or so, she would come over and tidy up from top to bottom and berate me for letting it get into a mess.

My memories would haunt me every night, so I didn't sleep. They just kept going around and around in my head. I used to take sleeping tablets to help me get just a few hours' respite. It would work for a little while but then I used to take more to get the same effect. The tablets would make me drowsy during the day. This was a vicious cycle that I got myself in. I never really knew what time of the day it was; I used to turn up to things late or not at all. Everything was a huge effort.

I am being completely honest with you by telling you all the details because if I can help others to say NO and get out of their situation, then I will feel better about myself. Some kids think that abuse in the home by supposed loved ones is normal. These people - paedophiles - need be stopped. I have spent years with it all going around and around in my head until I have felt like it was driving me mad. It needs to be said, I'm sorry. Exposing what he has done is what I have to do.

Exposing what is going on behind closed doors is a must. Abuse damages kids for generations down the line. It has got to stop!!

This book has been the first step in my recovery; being able to talk about what has happened is liberating. I know I have a long way to go but at last I feel that I am worth something and can make something of my life. So can you!

In March 2006, I met my current partner; in December 2006, we had a son. Being a parent the second time around has been amazing. Don't get me wrong, I love my eldest son but I had him at 18, fresh from years of abuse. Christopher grew up with ADHD but is okay now. He gave me a tough time when he was a child and I had just emerged from an awful painful traumatic childhood two years before. I just wanted somebody I could love and was mine alone. Jemma came along two years later; we also had our ups and downs. There have been times when I have failed her. My parenting skills have been hit and miss but I had no role models; I was not prepared for parenthood. I thought love would get me through. By the age of 21, I had two kids.

I often feel guilty about my lack of parenting skills but I have learnt that beating myself up about it will not get me anywhere. All I know is I basically was left alone to bring them up. Their dad was around but he wasn't there for me or them emotionally. Jemma knows what happened to me and she understands and supports me all the way. I love her to do death and would defend her, no matter what. When Jemma isn't around, I miss her.

This is painful writing this. Why doesn't my mum love me enough and care enough about me? Why does she go to bed every night with a man who raped me and hurt her kids?

Zach has been my second chance. Zach and his dad do everything together. It's lovely to see a proper nurturing and loving relationship between a parent and a child. Christopher was already 16 when I had Zach and we have a strained relationship because of other things but I know that I love him and would lay down my life for him.

I have let myself be treated like a doormat because that's all I knew. I was soiled, stupid, and used as trash. This is how I felt my whole life. I still have difficulties. I misinterpret people's intentions and I am so defensive. My hackles rise as soon as I hear criticism. I go off on one and the brick wall comes up. It's the fight or flight response.

I do question my partner about Zach and I follow them about, but my partner would never do anything. I can't help it. I have never told my partner how I feel because I don't know how to express myself. If I hear my partner telling Zach off, I'm there in two seconds asking what's going on. There is nothing to worry about but having a good dad who loves and spends time with a child because they want to is so weird and alien to me; I come from a different world in this respect. I find it hard to trust anyone.

Since Chris wrote this book, I have been able to let go and realise everyone is not out to abuse and I am able to let my partner and Zach have their time together. In actual fact, I sometimes get jealous! I'm letting go and learning to trust since the book was started. I have been able to tell my deepest darkest secrets. My stepmother told me I lied about my dad touching me, but Tracey, our stepsister, confirmed that he did abuse me. My stepmother Vivien told me I was evil for lying about my dad so I deserved everything I got. My stepfather Fred told me at age nine that I liked being touched because my own dad had done it. I told him I lied about my dad as that is what Vivien had told me. My stepfather took this info and twisted it and used it against me. He told me that as I had already lied, no one would believe me about him, and if I told anyone I would have to go back to Vivien! What could I do?

So because of this, he was able to touch me for years; I was so scared, alone and terrified. He continued the abuse until I was 12. One day, I just told him NO and that was it! I kept what he had done to me a secret until I was 16. He started making comments about my boobs and trying to touch them as he went past. I had to tell someone; I could not take it anymore.

My mother would never have done anything so I went to Chris and the police. But it was never taken any further. The case was dismissed.

When I reported it at 16, I remember sitting there with total strangers telling them what happened. Can you imagine telling a stranger, explicit graphic details about the abuse? It was like I was reliving it, I couldn't bring myself to tell them he had raped me. I thought if I told them about the other things, that would be enough. He told them that I had lied about my real dad and I think that is what got him off! Even now, that whole time is an awful terrible memory. I don't really want to go through that again.

I often have bad days and throw up when I am stressed. I get severe acid which makes me throw up blood. No, it's not self-inflicted; I don't purge. I think it's my body's way of dealing with the stress. I won't see a doctor about it. Am I still punishing myself for allowing that scum to touch me? Yes, I believe I am. This needs to change.

Writing this book has bought all of my siblings closer together and I finally trusted them enough to tell them about the rape and full extent of the abuse. I have love and support, not the horror and disgust I thought I would get. If you find yourself in a similar situation, please tell someone. If I had told someone the extent of the abuse years ago, he would have been sent down. I have felt degraded downtrodden and dirty for years. The abuse is not my fault; it is not your fault.

Can you see from my story what a burden has been lifted when I finally told others? I may do something about reporting Fred again one day, but for now I feel happier free and ready to live my life without guilt, despair or shame.

Don't get me wrong, I'm still broken. Some bits of my childhood were bleak and my mental and emotional health needs restoring. I am a jigsaw puzzle with missing bits. But I now know the bits can be found and put back together.

Thank you, Chris, from the bottom of my heart. Thank you for writing the book; it's helped me in leaps and bounds. I've realised that you have been there for me all my life. I don't have a brilliant mother, but she gave me you x

My younger brother, Michael (38)

So much has happened, Chris. Mum and Fred did so much stuff to me that I've forgotten most of it, but there are a few memories that really stand out.

One night, I woke up and needed a drink and he was pissed. I was half asleep and he pushed me down a flight of stairs for no reason, just because he could. I smashed my back into the post in the middle of the stairs. He told everyone I was sleepwalking and at the time I was too scared to say anything.

Another time, he lost it after coming back from the pub. He and Mum decided to start on me and they traded punches into me. It ended up with one of them smashing my head face first into the fridge. I fell to the floor and he put the boot in, over and over. I swore that day I'd get revenge.

From what I can remember, the beatings started for me almost as soon as I was there. Mum hated me. I could tell. She let me know all the time, "You look like your father," then she would beat me. At the time, I had a problem wetting the bed and she would grab my head and rub my face in the sheets, punching me. Then he would come in and she would bring him in and he would punch and kick me.

After a while, I couldn't take it. I used to hide the clothes. Sometimes throwing them away in the cubby hole underneath the stairs in the garden. I even once hid them and took them to school. I knew if I didn't, I would get beaten by Mum and him as soon as I got in!

When I went to senior school, the bed-wetting stopped (almost). I thought the beating would stop but they just found anything to beat me. If one of you older ones did anything, after you left I would get beaten for it. If the younger ones did anything, I would get it too.

I was afraid of Mum and Fred. I can remember having an accident and she said, "You want to be like a dog? You can live like one," and she tried to put me under the stairs with the dog. When I refused, she beat me. She hated me. Probably even more than him.

Then I left. I just couldn't take it anymore but I soon realised that I was quite strong and that I was going to have to stand up to him. I realised that after you all left. I got it. I realised that after I left, it would be our half-sister who got it, so after I heard about Di I just realised in my head I had to go back.

He was nice at first but I knew it was coming. One day he came in while I was reading a book and he knocked it into my face. I stood up and said to him, "Yeah?" And he suddenly backed down.

Not long after that, I moved out for good!

Many of you will know I took a lot of drugs then. Nothing I couldn't handle but I needed it.

I had problems. Nightmares of him every bloody night. Him hitting me and me not being able to get away. I swore to myself … one day …

Then Mum had her head thing. I really didn't want to go to that hospital but my friends said I might regret it and Andy said it might be the last time I saw her. I really hoped she would have the answers and then die. I'm not gonna lie.

She told me in that room when she thought she was dying that she was sorry and she did love me. I can't describe how that felt. But as soon as she came round after her operation, she asked for me and whispered to me, "I lied. You look like your father and I hate you." For her, that was it. To me, she was scum and she will always be scum.

I hated having to be in the same room as him at our half-sister's wedding. It made my blood boil. Then that surreal fight started. Mum fighting in the middle of the floor. I scanned the room. The only person not in there was Fred. As soon as I thought it, my jacket was off. It's probably the calmest I've ever been. As I swung the doors open to the other bar, there he was. Standing with three old blokes.

As I walked towards him, he tried to kick me but he missed. I jumped him and then I hit him as hard as I have ever hit anyone or anything. His teeth went up into his mouth and I knew I had properly hurt him. Then I rammed his head into the fag machine and then the bouncers stopped it! I knew then that was it. He no longer had a hold over me. Never again would he hit me. I was in charge. He was the scared man.

I've never had that nightmare since but I still hate him and her with a vengeance.

Then I realised I had to get away. When I'm angry, I don't know when to stop.

On a number of occasions, I've contemplated beating him to a pulp but something (or someone) has stopped me.

I thought I was fine with all this. But now? I had made a life for myself but all this makes me so angry. I've never had kids because I like to live and I've never felt well off enough.

The only thing I've realised is that I can't cry like normal people. Nothing makes me sad. I only cry when I'm getting angry.

Looking back, Mum was just as much an abuser as he was to me. Although what he did to Di? Well for that, he just pips her. I can live with most of the rest, but that gets me. I do know I hate them both with a vengeance. That is never going to leave me.

And when the day comes, I do intend to go to Mum's funeral. Just to make sure she's in the box!

Acknowledgements

Where do I start?

First I have to thank my family:

My husband Andy and my beautiful children, Ben and Charley.

My nan, Nanny 'Grunt' Freda, who saved us, my big brother David (Dave), my little sister Diane (Didi) and little brother Michael (Mick). Also my two half-sisters, who have expressed a wish to stay anonymous, and I think my mum. We all went through so much together.

My in-laws, Shelagh, Bob and Matt.

I also want to thank the people in my life who helped me in ways they perhaps might never know or understand.

The lady who gave me the apple every day at primary school; my school friends Louise Driscoll, Sarah Brand and their late mum Jo Driscoll; Susan Moorlen; Michelle Fairweather (for my taste in *Wham!* and fear of make-up); Arwen's mum, who helped me get the grant for catering college; Kathleen, Allison and Maureen, true friends; Sue Scourfield; Hazel Oliver; Carole Jeffery Bradshaw; Lisa Evans; Diane Horstead; Sally Sinclair; Lynn Dicken; Julie Maslin; Alison Winyard; Frances Malekos; Jan Spencer and Angie Munro, who put up with 11 years of my moaning at the Priory.

I also want to thank those people who have helped me with my business and personal development:

Jonathan Copp, for getting me through my Exercise to Music training; Ann Farwell, who taught me "If you are not happy, you need to follow your heart"; Rachel Holmes; Dax Moy, Mel Collie; Petra Rowden Harvey; Marc Kent; Chloe Stephens; Simon Jones; Austin Lawrence and Tanya Caffrey.

I just want to say a massive thank you to all these people and to all the other amazing people I've not mentioned. You have been pivotal in my life and have all played a massive role in making me, ME!

Last but not least; Karen Laing for helping me put all my memories together into a book that flows and makes sense!

Thank you for buying my book *Through the eyes of a child*. Some of the proceeds from your purchase is being re-invested into Survivors Of aBuse.org and will go towards providing professional help for survivors of abuse.

If you have any comments or feedback regarding this book, please can you email me at info@survivors-of-abuse.org
I would love to hear from you.

If you need help, please check out

http://www.survivors-of-abuse.org/

https://www.facebook.com/groups/SOBBTC/

Be true to yourself,

Chris

x

Lightning Source UK Ltd.
Milton Keynes UK
UKOW01f0315181115

262970UK00001B/44/P